The
40-Day
Warfare Plan
of
Binding and Loosing

Daniel and Sheila Brothers

ISBN 0-939241-86-2

Book Description

*T*his book is a strategic 40-Day Warfare Plan of binding the powers of darkness off the innocent people around us, while at the same time, loosing these victims from demonic grips for greater freedom in the Holy Spirit. **We are responsible** for those around us who think they see, but are blind indeed. This book is based on the Scriptures in Matthew 18:18-19, of binding and loosing, and wherever two or more are gathered together, and agree, it shall be done! Souls around us are going to hell in a hand basket, but now we can join together in warfare prayer, on specific dates, against specific demonic powers, and make a specific difference in the lives around us, as well as in our own. Jesus came to set the captives free...now He can use us...the common laymen...to set more captives free than ever thought possible. You are very aware that the problem is not with flesh and blood, but against the powers of darkness that blind and manipulate people. Now, here is at least one plan that can make a difference.

This Plan Has Three Parts:

(1) 40 days of binding a list of demonic names, and loosing your list of people for Greater Freedom.

(2) 40 days of Praise and Thanksgiving to the Father for deliverance, and Proxy Prayers for the lost, and for lukewarm Christians.

(3) 40 days of hands off...a time of doing nothing but resting in the Lord with faith, that He is manifesting changes in lives around us.

This 120-Day Plan can be done three times per year.

Not only will you be rebuking curses and praying healing for your list of people, but for others all around the world. On these specific dates, other prayer partners will be agreeing with you, your family, and your list, all at the same time. The power that will generate from all this agreement cannot and will not be possible to measure in this lifetime.

You can and WILL make a difference...are you ready?

Contents

Note:
Most bible translations I study are the King James Version and The Living Bible. Most Scriptures listed within this book will be taken from The Living Bible...only because it is easier to understand, not because it tis better than the King James Version.

CHAPTER 1

"Your Care for Others Is the Measure of Your Greatness!" (Luke 9:48, TLB)

*T*hose are the red letters of Jesus' very own words about one's greatness. It is in the caring for others and not in the turning against them. These words of His will probably shoot through your heart like daggers, as it has in mine. I'm sure it smote the disciples then as it still does today. The Word is sharper than a two-edged sword, but in the moment of pain that the scalpel brings, there is hope. Hope for healing through the deliverance of the cutting away. Only the mature can bear the scalpel face on. "Well done, thy good and faithful," will only be said to those who willfully walk forward into the Word's operating room. Jesus only spoke of that which was the most important to the Father for us. No idle words fell from His lips. The good news is...**there is hope for you and me, AS WELL AS THOSE AROUND US.** There is hope of getting free from the accuser who makes us focus on our failures all the time. Jesus does not condemn us; He wants to use us in the raging battle that surrounds us. Even though it may seem like people are going along in peace and contentment, **look around...it's a lie!** *Zombies look and act the same way,* I know, I was one. It's time to sound the alarm, and wake up the sleeper. This routine-rut life-style is just a grave with the ends knocked out. The Holy Spirit desires to shake up and wake up; He shook things in the beginning and He wants to again today. His presence and power always separates and divides the doer from the hearer only. So what if people get offended at warfare intercession. **So what**...once they wake up and see, they like Paul on the road to Damascus will become even greater. **The blinders are their problem...they just don't see!**

     Luke 9:49-50, TLB: **His disciple John came to him and said, "Master, we saw someone using your name to cast out demons. And we told him not to.**

After all, he isn't in our group." But Jesus said, "You shouldn't have done that! For anyone who is not against you is for you."

Jesus clearly rebukes the disciples into awareness by shocking their eyes open to the fact that He does work through others outside of their puny religious circle. Jesus was also pointing out the fact that others were seeing the power for deliverance from demons in His name. This should be a common thing happening through believers, and that they should be glad for others because they are helping the causes of Christ...not hindering them. Setting victims free from Satan's grip is the first priority, and if not, then we are hindering the Gospel message. Ouch! That hurts! I'm bleeding. I better go to the Red Cross and get a **Band-Aid of Grace! Grace!** There is forgiveness for the past, and grace for the future. Thank You, Father, in Jesus' name!

This message is FREEDOM, just like William Wallace proclaimed in the *Brave Heart* movie...**not religion, and compromise!** Taking back stolen ground in people's lives from these ungodly trespassers is the high calling of all those **who will listen.** Heaven doesn't want religion...heaven wants to fight...fight for freedom...sever the enemy...set the captives free...charge...go forward...and never...never...**n.e.v.e.r. retreat!** So, what are we waiting for? We are all dressed up in the Word and **now** there is somewhere to go.

Intercession

There is a law between our Lord and Satan's kingdom, that prevents their interference with our will, but they both move in response to the actions of their followers. When we call out to the powers above, good or evil, it will be interpreted as green lights for action by either one. In all reality, both are activated, because one is trying to work their works, while the other one is trying to block the opposing force. **The battle is for our will.** The greatest battles are over our will of prayer and intercession, especially intercession, because it is greater than prayer.

Yes! Intercession is greater than prayer! Why? Because intercession is standing in the gap for others as more important than ourselves, while prayer is talking about our own needs and desires. Our motive behind our call will determine whether it is prayer or intercession. Solomon prayed for wisdom because his motive was to help the causes of God by helping the people. God gave him wisdom because he prayed to help others more than himself. Solomon also got the desires of his heart, and even far more, which Satan later used to trip him up.

Psalm 37:4 says to delight yourself in the Lord and He will give you the desires of your heart....Well then, what are we waiting for? If we see the problem, then the Father is saying to us, "What are you going to do about it?" Once we see, we pray for intercession to rise up within us and show us how to intercede properly, not haphazardly. He has a plan for victory in every situation. This is when we must pray for the mind of Christ in order to see what the Father is doing, and then intercede with His will of love and power. Love will bring His power, but power does not necessarily bring love. When we love His ways more than our own, then and only then, will His power manifest through our prayers and intercession.

This is how we work with Christ, not against him!

If you do not care about the captives, then you better start today, because you are on the enemy's hit list as well. Besides, love and concern is how you are like Christ, if you do not love, then you are not like Christ. This fruit is the true measure of our maturity in Christ likeness. Love is the measure of your greatness (Luke 9:48). Love and compassion is His plan of action for others. Therefore, He will equip us with this fruit as gifts if we only recognize our lack, and cry out for more. Doesn't love cover over a multitude of sins? Then pray to the God of love for more of Himself (1 Peter 4:8). To rule in love as a mediator between the injustice of good and evil in people's lives, is His number one purpose for our existence on earth...as it is in heaven.

*Help us God! Use Your branding iron on us, and burn
Your purposes deep within our hearts and wills.*

Salvation Testimony

One Arkansas Saturday night in May of 1976, at 2 a.m., I knelt down in front of my TV set with Oral Roberts, and said the sinners prayer for salvation. I then looked up and said, "Jesus, if You're real, then prove Yourself to me personally, and be more real to me than just the words of some man." His presence instantly came upon me with love, repentance, forgiveness, and freedom from a guilty conscience all rolled up in one, as my eyes flowed with many tears that beautiful spring night of being born again. Jesus had become Savior of my soul that night, but it took until August to understand that Jesus also wanted to be Lord of my life. That was when I got water baptized in Eugene, Oregon. Making Him Lord meant that I must put His desires first in everything. Realizing that I needed more of Him to do this properly, I sought Him for the baptism of His Holy Spirit, which He soon did. The more I grew in the Lord, the more I could see the problem in the bigger picture that hinders good from evil in mankind, as well as in myself. I realized that living at the altar on Sunday morning wasn't getting me free from mood swings of anger, depression, frustration, criticism, sickness, and a number of other things that had their way with me and those around me from time to time. I had to know more!

Demons in Believers

Through the help of books, friends and the Holy Spirit, I realized that demons do affect Christians, mostly stemming from generational curses that we have become victims of through years of lack of knowledge. I always argued that Christians could not have demons and the Holy Spirit at the same time, but I could see that something was coming out that was not God, and it was far more than just the flesh. **I learned that Christians *can have* demons, but not total possession, as in having the Holy Spirit, but not possessed by Him either.**

Battle for Our Peace .

I finally understood that this is why all the turmoil was going on inside me, because the war between good and evil was fighting for my peace. My peace is where evil used to live in me through the deception of false security. Upon being born again, I had now opened myself up for the peace that surpasses all understanding through the Holy Spirit's abiding presence; but this only made the rage of battle intensify. You see, **it's His peace in us that makes us strong,** and everything outside of this peace is a foothold for evil in us. Our peace is like a pie that the evil one is trying to steal a slice back, so he can infect the whole thing, just like a bad apple spoils the whole bunch. When we lose our peace, we also lose God's presence during that time, and we will usually make a wrong decision during that time as well. Only by guarding His peace in us, can we make His correct decisions because He speaks in that still small voice that is peaceful and calming. Words and situations cause feelings to respond, which cause decisions to be made, which make actions manifest in ways that we will have to repent of if they are outside of peace. Being still and knowing that God is God, will anchor your faith on the Rock of Peace that will resist the devil and cause him to be put under your feet, and flee for a time. Upon seeing this great need for peace and the constant frustration of this up and down Christian walk, going from victory to failure, with no steady stability, I sought out deeper truth in Christ than I was now receiving.

Deliverance in Atlanta and Texas

Seeing the problems that demons can manifest in a professing believer, my wife and I sought out a specialist in this field, just like any other special field. We found a man in Atlanta, Georgia, that did deliverance in his home. Arrangements were made for deliverance with him on our way to Texas to minister at some churches. As soon as we sat down on his couch, I started yawning. He said I was getting deliverance already. I quickly explained that it was just the trip from Charlotte, North Carolina. He

4

smiled, and began explaining how demons can enter us through the womb from childhood to adulthood through generational curses, witchcraft, fears, unbelief, worries, rejection, spoken curses, anger, depression, confusion, sex, sickness, diseases, and many other spirits that open up doors for evil to build their strongholds in our lives. It was up to us to humble ourselves and confess these things as sin that we allowed to dwell there and openly confess them and exposing them to the Light. We had to repent and renounce any and all things that were not of the Holy Spirit, and ask for forgiveness, which we quickly did.

Jesus desires to free us when we renounce them and cover them in His blood, because He sees us as victims of spirits that deceive us into giving them our wills, which manifest themselves through our flesh. We are like lions with thorns in our feet and sides. The lion is not the enemy, but the thorns are, since they make us behave in ways contrary to the Father's will. Some day our lion nature will lie down in peace and contentment, instead of being selfish and harmful like a flesh eater; until that day when we will actually be seated with Christ in the heavenlies. The battle of the thorns are ever present in the work of deliverance. Spiritual surgeons are needed to recognize the difference between the person and the thorns of torment, and lovingly extract the thief of peace, so that healing and freedom can restore man's peace of mind, body, and emotions of his soul. No believer can truly say that he sees, until he sees mankind as the victim, instead of the enemy. Once again, we war not against flesh and blood, but against the powers and principalities of evil that are constantly buzzing around in the airways over mankind, looking for a loophole to get in and manifest their purposes, instead of the rightful owner themselves.

Unforgiveness

Unforgiveness is the biggest problem in receiving any kind of deliverance, because it is Satan's greatest loophole into our lives, since unforgiveness blocks our prayers from being answered (Matt. 18:34-35, Mark 11:25-26).

We learned that **unforgiveness was and is the number one hindrance to answered prayers,** as well as getting free from tormenting spirits. It was necessary to forgive others in the past all the way to childhood, and to forgive God Himself, because of blaming Him for things and the way He made us, while having to forgive ourselves for failures and self-hatred. Forgiveness was mostly an act of will, because we didn't feel it in some cases. We later felt real forgiveness when the spirit of unforgiveness was cast out; no wonder we couldn't feel it before, a spirit was behind it all. *If we will not humble ourselves and forgive, then we will be turned*

over to the corrector, for the saving of our souls (Matt. 18:35). The greater the offense against us, the greater the love it takes to forgive, by turning our cheek. Jesus did it constantly because He loved the Father, and so must we. **Forgiveness proves our love** to Jesus and the Father, like nothing else. **Demons hate you when you forgive, because it shakes their legal hold in your lives.**

Calling Out Spirits

After the initial renouncing, forgiveness, and praying, the Atlanta man started calling out spirits by name and binding them here on earth as they are bound in heaven; and loosing deliverance upon us through the blood of Jesus in the Holy Spirit's presence. I started yawning real big yawns with tears, while my wife yawned and coughed. He later said they can come out through yawning, blowing, coughing, burping, crying, yelling, vomiting, gas, screaming, and runny noses. **Deliverance is said to be for the desperate,** and desperate we were, and out they came with feelings of relief flowing in.

Humble Thyself

When we humbled ourselves before a brother and said, **"If there's anything in us that grieves the Holy Spirit, we want it out."** That attitude was the straw that broke the devil's stronghold in our lives, and it will be for anyone that humbles themselves and says those words. We sat there for over two hours getting free from junk. Some demons of disease and affliction started manifesting openly to the point that they were arguing with the man. He commanded them to cough out, and leave the premises and go to the abyss. When he got ahold of another big one in my wife, I grabbed my video camera and captured five different demons of sickness leaving her. If I hadn't seen them leave this woman, who walked with God for 32 years, with many personal miracles, I would not have believed it myself.

Texas

On our way to Texas the next day, we discussed in length what we should do with this newfound revelation, but God had it all planned out for us. The day after our arrival, our Pentecostal pastor friend, asked what we thought about demons in Christians. After our shock, we explained our story and showed him the videotape. He said the golden phrase, **"If there is anything in me that grieves the Holy Spirit, I want it out."** He asked if we could do deliverance on him, and we said we could if the Lord was willing; since the Atlanta man had prayed for us to receive the impartation for deliverance.

Note: We later learned that it is not really an impartation as much as it is a commandment for all believers to cast out demons (Mark 16:14-18).

After taking him through repentance and forgiveness, big demons began to manifest themselves to us, and argued that they would not leave their home. They confessed how many times they had tried to kill him, and they would win if we would leave them alone. These demons laughed at us and tried to scare us away, but we didn't move an inch, staying in their face and commanding them to leave in Jesus' name and by His blood. I knew that this man would not believe this when it was all over, so I put the camera on him for over two hours. After he coughed out spirits of bondage, pride, and lust, he was smiling with newfound freedom. Needless to say, this started us into two full weeks of deliverance for a bunch of believers in that area. When we returned home, we continued the work and helped many get delivered, as well as doing deliverance in their homes and churches.

Deeper Deliverance Needed

During that year of 1991, working with many believers caught up in their tangle of demonic webs, we were realizing more and more that a one-time deliverance was not a quick fix answer, because many demons could get back in through our will that yielded to the flesh. We realized that people needed to be continually set free from certain spirits that kept harassing them. We saw that self-deliverance was very powerful because the owner of their temple along with the Holy Spirit, were the main authorities. Just like in the natural laws, we are the main authority in our own homes, and have the legal right to cast out whom we don't want in, or on our premises. Self-deliverance became a powerful tool in combating the enemies' plans for ourselves, while at the same time doing more deliverance for others and gaining more personal freedom.

Self-deliverance information is following.

Self-deliverance seemed great for a while, but it wasn't enough just to get loose from things that plagued us, while seeing nonbelievers dying and going to hell because of unbelief in Christ (Eph. 4:18, Psalm 107:10-20). I knew that demonic powers had people blinded to the love and blood sacrifice of Christ, through their powers of darkness, deception, lying, confusion, unbelief, false religions, and many other spirits that kept them from seeing the Light. I knew there must be an answer somehow, somewhere, and once again...

Necessity Is the Mother of Invention.

CHAPTER 2

40-Day Revelation and Lists

California Letter

*T*his problem was perplexing and oppressing, until July of 1993. I listened to a local pastor read a letter that he received from his pastor friend in California.

The California pastor told how one day he and his wife were having their separate quiet times on a secluded beach, when a huge swarm of flies came upon them in such mass that it really startled them both. Knowing that Satan is Beelzebub, lord of the flies, he searched the library for information on flies in order to enlighten their experience. The fact he found most interesting was that to exterminate flies from an area, *you must disinfect it daily for 40 days.* **He realized that Satan was a short-term fighter, and that if we can resist him and his foe for 40 days, then he will have to leave us for a time, just like he did Jesus in the wilderness.** Luke 4:1

Bells and whistles went off in my head. I knew that this was the answer for the people in my world that I'm responsible for. You see, I already knew that I wasn't responsible for the whole world, but I was responsible for the world around me that I revolved in on a daily basis first, then the world at large. You see, I believe that we, like King David, have been chosen to cover in prayer and warfare, any and all people that the Lord has put into our care for protection. If we are found to be an irresponsible hireling, instead of a loving shepherd over our flocks when He returns, then heads will roll up yonder...probably ours! (John 10:13).

If you are truly born again, then you have a flock to pray over and care for. If you laugh about caring for others, then you probably have a spirit of indifference, which steals, kills, and destroys love and compassion; which in turn makes us all just a self-centered tinkling sound...good for nothing for Christ's purposes. It is possible to become so heavenly minded in seeking the things of God in self-gratification and self-righteousness, that we will become of no earthly good. The Pharisees, like Paul before his true conversion, were **heavenly minded, but of no earthly good,** because they did not care about man's needs. Jesus showed them the Way, the Truth, and the Life, through practical example, but they couldn't see through the "glass darkly" because of their blinders of pride and self-centeredness. We must humble ourselves, pick up our cross of Christ's purposes, and do the works of Him who sent us. If not, then can we truly say that we love Jesus as our Savior and our Lord? Do not let the enemy accuse you even at this very moment with feelings of failure and disappointment. **Get mad! Get mad!** Get mad at the way these bullies have been pushing you around. The Holy Spirit will convict you, if you are mature enough to hear it, but He will not accuse you as worthless. **You are not worthless.** You are heaven's only hope of setting the captives free, by starting today.

Hallelujah, Lord Jesus...Yes! Amen!

Anyway, back to my story...I got off on a rabbit trail there....

Revelation and List #1 (List of People)

After I stopped spinning around with revelation about the 40-day extermination plan, I came up with two lists. One list had all the names of people I could think of. I let each person's name be the source of contact for the whole family instead of trying to get every name. I'm believing that ten generations on both sides of each person's name will be touched through warfare prayer, even their spouse and their bloodline back to ten generations; even their ex-spouses, since they had a soul tie with them (Acts 16:31, Acts 11:14, Deut. 23:3). This may seem like a lot of people represented by one name in a family, but I am not going to be found guilty for not believing God for the impossible.

If we think it probable, God will make it possible.

I questioned God one day if this was crazy, and could I really let one name represent so many people like a tribe. The instant thought that came to me was, *"Wasn't I able to choose the first born of all the Egyptians and their livestock?"* (Exodus 11:5).

I was then done with the spirits of doubt and unbelief accusing me about God's inability. Spirits only have to get us to doubt God, not make us believe it. Doubt will open the door wide enough for unbelief to come in, then confusion, then depression, and then hopelessness comes in and opens the door wider for frustration to take root, thus making a seed bed for murmuring and complaining to spring forth, and cause ourselves to be turned over to the tormenter for correction, for the saving of our souls. Praising the Lord in all things is more for our protection and prevention from opening the wrong doors, than it is to just flatter God. Doors once opened can also become shut again, as we backtrack and repent, and bind them shut by rebuking them in Jesus' name, and covering them with His blood.

Spirits hate each other, but they will work together in order to control their victims. Their ultimate goal is not only to cause us to be a laughingstock in the face of God, but to make us lose heart in God's Word to the point of despair, opening up opportunities for death and suicide to manifest themselves into actions of self-murder; where there is no forgiveness after the fact. They know that they are destined for hell, and they want to take us with them, while preventing us from helping others find the Way. They are succeeding in many, but we have the authority in Christ to say, **"No more devils, loose my people in Jesus' name."** We must work together, in order to loose them into freedom of life, and life more abundantly. He is more than able to carry our faith no matter how big or small it may be. Matthew 17:20...mustard seed faith.

PART 1

(Clarification of the three parts...the four lists, and their procedures, are coming up soon.)

List #2 (Warfare List — Demons and Commands)

This is the first part of 40-day warfare.

My **#2 list** was made up of every kind of demonic spirit I could think of. You see, I believe that *if it is not of the Holy Spirit, then it is of another spirit.* So I listed spirits of emotions, mental, sexual, abusive, curses, false religions, sickness, temptations, and many more that are listed in the following pages. It came up to many pages of demons, along with Scriptures and commands of warfare authority. Six days a week, Monday through Saturday, I would read my list out loud, which took about 20 minutes (about 45 minutes now) mornings seemed best because of binding demons for the day; and mornings have fewer distractions, which hinder all serious closet prayer times. Sometimes it was delayed, and started as late as 11:59 p.m., but I always **started** it before midnight. Since nobody was agreeing with me in this, I made a pact that I would start all over again if I missed one day during a 40-day siege against the enemy strongholds. I only called out the list of demons and commands for six days a week, Monday-Saturday. On Sunday I would rest from warfare and read off my **Praise and Thanksgiving List (list #3)** and call out the names on my people list. Not praying individually for them, unless the Lord quickened someone. I just called them out to the Lord like lifting them up as an offering to Him to have His way in their lives. It would usually take about 20-30 minutes, also depending on how many people I had listed. I found, as you will, that more people were added to my #1 list, as well as demons were to my #2 list.

That is six days of warfare, one day of praise, repeated each week, for a total of 40 consecutive days. My #3 list, for Sunday's praise and thanksgiving, was and is just a heartfelt gratitude for God's power of deliverance; along with some proxy prayers for those who may not be able to pray for themselves yet.

Demons Under Every Bush?

If you hear a voice that says to you, "You must not give too much attention to the devil, and look for demons behind every bush," ask yourself, **"Is that the Holy Spirit that sounds scared?"** *I don't think so!* You see, Scriptures say that we are to be as gentle as a dove (keep your peace), but wise as a serpent (Matt. 10:16). That means that we should be as smart as he is and know his plans so we can foul them. Besides, Jesus Himself commanded the disciples to preach, to cast out, and to heal. **That was His focus of attention and that better be ours as well** (Mark 16:17). Wars in the natural are examples of how we should war in the Spirit. Knowing our enemy plans, and our weapons, will always help us win battles and set the captives free. I would not want to be in a foxhole with a soldier that was not intent on searching the bushes for the enemy, and so it is in the Spirit.

Give me a troop of believers with eyes wide open, and watch the enemy forces flee!

The Lord can work through those who truly see and stay awake, but the only hope for the sleeper is repentance from their dead works in Christ.

David ruled 40 years over the natural.

I was also doing these forty days like King David ruled for 40 years. He ruled over the natural but we must rule over the spiritual. He was both a man of God and of war, so must we, but only against the powers of darkness.

PART 2

List #3...*40 Days of Praise and Thanksgiving*

After I did the first 40 days, I asked the Lord, "What should I do next?" My thoughts turned to how Solomon reigned 40 years in praise and peace, while blessing the people that he was responsible for. So, I started another 40 days of reading out loud my **#3 praise and proxy list** on the six days, and just calling out the people's names **(list #1)** on Sunday. This went along just fine until I got to the end of those 40 days.

PART 3

(No List)...*40 Days of Hands Off...Do Nothing*

"Lord, what now?" The more I meditated on it, the more I realized that after Solomon's reign, the kingdom split up. Two tribes went with the king of Judah, while ten tribes went with the king of Israel (II Chron. 11:1). It was a kind of "let them go and see what they do"; so I called it a time of **hands off.** Forty days of doing nothing, but wait, watch, and see what happens to the people on my lists. It's a time to let go and see what truth is established in each person, while resting in faith that the Lord is doing a deeper work inside by letting junk come to the surface and being exposed. Make notes of what is manifesting in people's lives during this time, so that these spirits can be beat on during the next round of binding and loosing.

40 days of warfare
40 days of praise
40 days of hands off
Total of 120 days...which equals 1 ROUND

List #4...*Spoils List*

During this whole time of 120 days, I had another list, which I called my praise report list, or spoils list. It was a record of any kind of report I received about anyone on my list, good or bad. During the first 40 days, the reports were, and usually will be, bad things happening because of the "Battle of Deliverance," similar to that of Moses and Pharaoh. I need to find a theologian that can tell me how many days Moses wrestled with Pharaoh; I would not be surprised if it was 40 days.

Moses Interceded

I know one reason why God called Moses. It was because he probably prayed and interceded for Israel all those 40 years in the desert. His failed attempt greatly enhanced his groaning for his forgiveness, and for their deliverance. Now that was some serious intercession for sure. Moses spent 40 years in the wilderness and Christ spent 40 days in the wilderness. Surely we can call out 40 days in intercession of binding and loosing for the blind, deaf, wretched, lost, dying, and poor in Spirit.

120 days x 3 times a year = 360 DAYS = 3 ROUNDS

The amazing thing that I realized was that I could do this 120-day warfare plan, three times in a year with five days left over. "But what was I to do with those five days, Lord?" Oh yes, one day goes between each block of 120 days, which uses up three days, and I guess the last two days will be for Christmas and Easter, which won't be included in the 40 days. So, there you have it, **three 120-day periods with five spaced out days of rest.**

A PAGE OF DETAILED DATES ARE FOLLOWING

This plan is not a law

Above all...believe this...this plan of mine is not a law that must be followed to the letter. It's just one battle plan of many that I believe the Lord wants to use to set His people free. If days are missed, just say, **"Grace, Grace,** in Jesus' name," and go on with it, especially when others are doing this list with us at the same time. We will be holding up each other's arms as they did for Moses. When you tire out, just sit on the rock, and let others hold you up (Ex. 17:12). This is just a battle plan to start an attack with. You can add to it or take away from it. *It's just a start,* and that is **all we need.** We have to start somewhere, so why not **here and now.**

Specific dates are assigned

You can do this anytime you desire, but I've listed specific days that will be continually used from this day forward, so that partners around the world that wish to join forces can all start together and be in one accord. *Wow! Around the world...? Wow! And wow again!* Can you imagine people all around the world binding and loosing in warfare intercession...all of us being of one mind and one joint action, to the pulling down of strongholds over people's lives? **That's an amazing thought...*you represent them, and they represent you.* It's kind of like a *giant pen pal prayer group,* WOW!** You see, I'm basing this whole battle plan on two verses: **Matthew 18:18-19...where two or more are gathered to-gether and agree on anything in Jesus' name, they will receive it; and whatever we bind on earth will be bound in heaven, and whatever we loose on earth, will be loosed in heaven.** There are many more Scriptures for my faith in this battle plan, but these are the two main ones that I stake everything on.

You Will Be on Many Lists!

It is hard to imagine how much power God will generate when we join together in corporate prayer of binding and loosing. The greatest blessing for those who do this plan, on the assigned days listed, will have everyone warring for them each day as well. The plan covers not only you and your list of people, but also covers the lists of your prayer partners around the world. People will be covering you in a greater way than you ever could all by yourself. That is the point: *Pray for others as more impor-tant than yourself, and see God bless you more and more,* without having to pray so hard for yourself. We get covered by covering others**...we reap more than we sow...what a deal!**

Lives Will Shake

I have found in the past that things start shaking in the lives of those on my list, but that is good. It is wrestling with principalities and powers of darkness that makes things shake. These reports will encourage you to go full steam ahead, because you will be seeing the power of warfare intercession at work. It will put a hope in your soul and a joy of expectancy in your attitude of increased faith. You do not have to tell anyone what you are doing over them unless they need the hope of breaking through, and **seeing the light at the end of the tunnel.**

Spoils List #4

Your spoils list are the same as when King David and the other kings went to war and won the battles. They got the goodies left behind by the enemy (I Chron. 26:27, II Chron. 20:25). In our case, the spoils will be the happiness here and the eternal rewards of those lost souls getting free from Satan's deception and receiving the light of Christ's salvation. Not only does this work on lost souls, but many believers will get free from their entanglements that hold them bound.

Freedom to see

Freedom is the purpose for the charge into the enemy camp. **Freedom was, and still is, the heart of Christ for us all.** We must work with our Lord while there is still daylight for the harvest (Matt. 9:37-38).

> **Oh, Children of the Light who say they see...**
> **P.L.E.A.S.E. help me set the captives free.**

The Help Us Fight Prayer

Will we say, "Yes, Lord, we hear You calling us to pick up our cross and bear Your arms...it was You who drafted us. We didn't choose You; it was **You who chose us.** Since You drafted us, Lord, we know that You will train us up in higher ways than our own, and You will lead us as we march with You in one accord. We war not with flesh and blood, but against principalities and powers that You overcame for us. So, now we must fight the good fight that You fought, against demonic powers with Your name and Your blood, in order *to loose those who cannot see.* It is only Your might and power that will bring freedom, and it is **You in us** that we count on for these victories. It's our willingness to follow, and Your strength to lead us, while keeping us in all Your ways."

> *Anoint us...*
> *Empower us...*
> *Oh Lord!*
> *PLEASE....*

CHAPTER 3

The Secret Training Ground

*T*he children in the wilderness were not prepared for battle because of being slaves for so many years in Egypt. The wilderness became a secret training ground for warfare preparation. **The old saying, "You can't teach an old dog new tricks,"** was the result of trying to recruit and train old mindsets with their fears and unbelief. The generation of that time was freed in body through God and Moses, but they were still in prisons of brainwashed feelings and beliefs of negativism. Years of depression and despair formed a grave-like rut of hopelessness and unbelief that they could not climb out of. Their engrained fears were magnified when they saw the enemy's strength and compared it with their lack of warfare training. Their self-doubt opened wide the doors for doubt in God's ability to save them. This doubting and complaining generation was basically erased from the blackboard of God's purposes. It took 40 years to school and train a troop of warriors in physical abilities, as well as to reestablish a new mind-set of hope and faith. I'm sure their training skills were limited at first because of unskilled trainers, but as time increased, so did their ability to fight. As their confidence grew, so did their faith in God's ability to use them in battle. Before they could fight the real enemy, they only had each other to practice against. Fine, if done in brotherly love, but if done in anger or frustration, then only civil war and division. Iron does sharpen iron, if done to help instead of hurt. Warring against flesh and blood through friendly fire was not God's purpose then, nor is it today. Friendly fire can help train the weak and fearful into a fighting force through edification, exhortation, and rebukes, if their heart is to humbly help and not to hinder.

The hope of Moses, as well as Christ, is to bring the people through, and into the Father's Promised Land Purposes. People are relying on the help of those who say they see and understand, but do we really? We fight each other and bury our wounded, while the enemy watches on in glee. It is time to blow the Shofar Horn, and wake each other up for the battle cry. It is time to turn this boat around and fight the currents of ease and comfort that lullaby the unconcerned asleep as they float along the rivers of unbelief, unaware of the falls of death and destruction ahead. Helping others was the call of God then and it still is today. We are required to intercede like Moses and fight like Joshua in this last day's battle. Bringing in the new, while weeding out the old. The Lord is doing the same thing in us as well...that is, for those who are yielding enough to bend their preconceived notions and get free from their old dog attitudes. Like it or not, wilderness boot camps are for us as well. We have the choice to prepare for warfare or to just go along for the lust of the promise land. Warriors will stay alert for opportunities to get over on the enemy, while the less attentive just focus on how quickly they can settle in. The problem with settlers is that they have a tendency to compromise into complacency and join the customs of the neighboring country's idol worship (worldly gratification), pulling down the rest (Judges 2:1-4). Compromise and fear is not, and was not, the attitude of Moses or William Wallace in the *Brave Heart* movie. We are to train and focus on warfare against the enemy without thought of our own personal comforts until everyone can rest in peace. The true and faithful ones *are not* busy holding meetings as to who is the most important or why the warriors should be doing it a different way. The lazy and selfish, always reveals themselves by their many words and little action. It takes a brave heart to do this plan, because it goes against the grain of the compromising settlers that are trying to settle in and get their unearned portions. In this warfare plan, the little old gray haired ladies will probably outfight those who think they stand pretty tall and strong...like Saul.

It's time to shake lose from the worldly cares and distraction that create weakness of faith and laziness of spirit. The Lord is depending on us to shake free, and set others free, without fear of man's opinions. Every generation has its called warriors to guard and to protect. Warriors are frustrated when songs of peace-peace are being sung while the enemy is building up their forces of destruction. We can't dance around in false security that everything is just fine, when the Christian body is being knocked around into weakness and unfruitfulness. Churches full of people are not the sign of spiritual prosperity...it's their freedom. Not freedom to jump around and shout, but freedom to help other lost and hurting souls get freedom for themselves. How can we truly be content when so many souls are going to hell everyday? How can we write them off as the rebellious ones, and turn our attention to the lusts of the world?

How much stuff do we need to make us happy in our false security and false peace...which is only a smoke screen for us to justify our busy lives as being too busy to help the hell bound get free? We are one of two types of people...warriors or settlers!

Warriors are not focused on settling,
and settlers are not focused on warring.

It's no wonder why there is so much strife in the body. The doers are shaking things, while the hearers only sit around complaining and murmuring. I know that these are strong words, but don't blame me...Jesus' Words always stepped on toes, and wounded egos. How can we be like Him and not proclaim His truths like Him? I am just writing down what comes to mind, with the belief that the Holy Spirit is helping me reveal His thoughts of love and correction.

Does harsh reality make you want to chunk this book in the garbage, or maybe just lay it down for a while? Of course it does! But it's too late...you can't get away from it now. The hook is in your stomach. You know it is time to get on with it. You want to be told the truth, even though it hurts the flesh. You have been looking for more in Christ than that which you are now getting from your routine life-style. The seed of loving warfare for others has been planted deep within your soul, and it will germinate into life, and life more abundantly. Just say, "Holy Spirit...please fertilize Your seed within me, and make loving others flower into a fruitful garden where we can fellowship in the cool of the day.

"Till my hardened soil of all its weeds. Produce a fruitful yield for the hungry, the weak, and the dying. Make my life in You, a life of giving even a cup of cold water to the parched and cracked lips of the thirsty that are already dry because of the flames of hell that are so near to them. Make me a living sacrifice of taking up my cross, for the purpose of setting the captives free.

"Please Lord...PLEASE!"

I bind, rebuke, and command all thoughts of failure and condemnation off you readers, in Jesus' name!

Idle Words...Blessings or Curses

Jesus said that we are either helping Him or hurting Him.
In Matthew 12:29-30, TLB: "One cannot rob Satan's kingdom without first binding Satan. Only then can his demons be cast out! Anyone who isn't helping me is harming me." In verses 31-37, Jesus clearly explains that our words have the power to help His causes and our fruitfulness, or our

damnation....**Our every idle word will judge us on judgment day. Our words now reflect our fate then** (Matt. 12:31-37).

This is a good place to swallow deeply and sigh grievously.

You see we are created in God's image to see, hear, think, and **create,** but the most powerful, yet deadly reality, **is our gift to create curses or blessings.**

Our words do create action that manifests in the airways around us to help or to harm. Idle words must become our **BIGGEST FEAR,** because they will come back upon us as blessings or curses, as well as on others. Spoken words are evidence of that which is created and manufactured in the heart. Repentance gives us forgiveness through the Blood of Jesus, but it's not dead works that should be our constant focus of attention, but the going on into the **greater works of maturity;** helping Christ in His cause of binding and loosing the powers of darkness...setting the captives free!

Say..."Yes, Amen Brother...Times Awasting!"

The Basic Ministry

In Matthew 10:7-42, TLB, Jesus commissions the 12 disciples with the basic ministry.

1. Go and announce to them (the blind in spirit) that the Kingdom of Heaven is near **(preach the gospel).**
2. Heal the sick, raise the dead, cure the lepers **(pray healing).**
3. And cast out demons **(do deliverance).**
4. Give as freely as you have received **(freely give).**
5. Be selfless about your own needs...(9-10) **(be selfless).**
6. Join in agreement with other believers (11-13) **(join believers).**
7. Be wise as serpents, yet peaceful as doves...(16) **(be smart and humble).**
8. You'll be arrested...persecuted...(17-18) **(persecution comes).**
9. Worry not what to say, be a witness...(19) **(worry not).**
10. The Holy Spirit will speak through you...(20) **(speak His words).**
11. Your loved ones will betray you...(21-25) **(expect betrayal).**
12. Don't be afraid of threats of death (26, 28) **(fear nothing).**
13. Hear my voice and proclaim from housetops (27) **(speak boldly).**
14. Your worth more than a sparrow...(29-31) **(trust God's love).**
15. Publicly acknowledge Jesus...don't deny Him (32-33) **(confess Jesus).**
16. Jesus causes family divisions...(34-36) **(expect divisions).**
17. Love Jesus more than others...(37-38) **(don't compromise).**
18. Lose your life in order to save it...(39) **(die to self).**

19. Welcome God by welcoming the godly...(40) **(welcome godly).**
20. Receive a prophet and receive his reward (41) **(receive equal reward).**
21. Be rewarded for giving even water, in Jesus (42) **(tiny gifts rewarded).**

Preach the Gospel, pray for healing, and do deliverance, while freely giving from selfless motives. Join other believers in agreement, while being alert, wise, smart, yet humble. When persecution comes, don't worry. Speak out His Words boldly as you are betrayed by loved ones. Fear nothing as you trust in God's love, and confess Jesus as Lord. Divisions will come, but do not compromise in dying to self-gratification. As you welcome the godly, give even the tiniest gifts of helps in Jesus' name...you will be greatly rewarded.

We may pick and choose which parts of Christ's commission that we want to embrace, but I believe they are all important and put in this order on purpose. *Jesus taught this basic ministry by* **example first.** Then the disciples were sent out to become His examples as well.

Religion may say this was for the past, but does Jesus agree? **What Jesus starts, He finishes.** It is not over until He says, "Well done, thou good and faithful servant!"

Basic ministry must first start with...
Preaching, Healing, and Deliverance.

If these are not our main priorities in walking with Christ as it was the disciples, then our motives are less than His and probably self-centered. I know this hurts, but we must judge ourselves now or be judged later. In the latter days, man will run to and fro looking for teaching that tickles their ears...that's today! (2 Tim. 4:3-4). The Word of God does cause division between darkness and light in our own souls, as well as in our relationships. It is sharper than a **TWO-EDGED SWORD,** dividing our thoughts and motives (Heb. 4:12). The Word sets us free if we truly hear and obey it, but our freedom is not enough. We must proclaim it over the captives, for their freedom as well.

Self-Sacrificing Love of
Jonathan and His Bodyguard

As well, means also, together in agreement, unity of thought, and in action. Agreement together is as powerful today as it was when Jonathan and his bodyguard took on the Philistines in *1 Samuel 14:1-46.* They joined together in a simple fleece agreement as to whether or not to go up and fight the enemy single-handed...with

God's miraculous help, of course. A miracle was what they were asking God for. They were seeking His will and not their own. They were willing to lay down their lives for the cause of helping God's people, **more than their own.** They were looking for God to do a bigger work than what they were used to seeing. Stepping out into giant killing takes the anointing; and blessed are those who reach out for it. **They tested God's will in verses 9-10,** by giving Him a chance to show Himself mightily in this fight. In verse 11, they heard the enemy voice say, **"Come on up here and we'll show you how to fight,"** but they understood it to be God's will for a miracle. Darkness always speaks lies, because the truth is not in him (Satan); so it was easy to **hear their negative prophecy, as God's positive prophecy.** The enemy voices are constantly speaking to us, but true discerning believers will recognize these lies as truth from the Lord. Satan knows the truth of God's will better than we do, so when the liar speaks...hear God. Jonathan heard and agreed with God as well as with his bodyguard. It was kind of a threefold cord is not an easily broken thing. If Jonathan had shared his new plan with others, they would have discouraged him and hindered God Himself. Woe to those who trip the faith of the little ones. In **verse 6,** Jonathan says, **"It doesn't matter how many enemies there are."** Neither did it matter how few *they* were either. Many are called, but few are chosen. Heroes are chosen today just as in days of old. Jonathan's battle plan was not according to the book of his times, *nor is this 40-day warfare plan,* but for all those who will agree together as the bodyguard said in **verse 7,** *"Fine, do as you think best; I'm with you heart and soul...whatever you decide!"* They, I'm sure, will see God do a miracle in their midst, wheeling the Sword of Truth, and cutting down the enemy forces in their arrogant pride and false security.

Jonathan and his bodyguard were examples of secretly done warfare intercession. No fanfare was given to these fearless ones until victorious results were seen by those standing around being religious and scared. *Jonathan had a desire in his heart* and heard God say, **"Yes,"** while Saul could not see the forest for the trees, and needed more confirmation before moving forward **(verses 17-19).** Saul finally did move out, when it was blatantly obvious that God was in it, yet he still had to put in his religious two cents of works and force everyone to fast in the fight. They probably had been fasting for some time already. That is why in **verses 31-34,** the men were hungry enough to eat raw meat. The simple faithful always seem to be the wiser as Jonathan did in **verses 29-30.** Saul was so religious that he was going to kill his own son for eating honey in the field, because Jonathan had broken *his law,* but not God's law. *Religious people will enforce their own rules as God's rules.* Their ways, as the only way. Their standards are lifted up higher than God's. They create a hoop of righteousness that they feel they can jump through, thus gaining the pride of self-righteousness and self-fulfillment. When we enforce something in order to obtain God's favor...*WE DON'T!* The greatest danger of becoming a hoop jumper is that it opens up doors for the Pharisee spirit to build us up, while belittling others as less. If Satan cannot keep us down through guilt, condemnation, and failure, then he will thrust us forward into the **same pride that made him fall from grace.**

It is always a good policy to pray for humility regardless of the level of spiritual maturity you have gained. We must humble ourselves before God, and ask Him to keep us humble or *pay the price of pride.* The truth is that if we cannot trust God enough to ask Him for humility and for patience, then we will receive pride and impatience...and God will resist them both (James 4:6).

Saul's dependence on religious works did not, and will not, bring about miracles like the simple childlike faith of Jonathan's total dependence of God, as to whether he lived or died. That was the same dependence David had on God all his life. That was what made him the apple of God's eye, and there is still plenty of room in God's eye for you and me.

Even though there may be few who start this fight, many more, even the fearful ones, will crawl out from their hiding places of false security, get on the band wagon, and fight the good fight of faith as they see some commotion for Hope of Victory, as in **verses 20-22.**

These Old Testament stories are not here just for bedtime reading. No! They are here as examples for us to fight in the Spirit as they fought in the natural.

David's Psalms of Enemies

In reading the Psalms of David, we see that David was always wrestling with flesh and blood as his enemies. The New Testament, that is in force today through the Blood of Jesus, commands us to love our enemies and not return judgment of an eye for an eye. So, in reading the Psalms today for proper focus, we must insert demons and sin, instead of people in those places where David rails against them; if not...then we will become accusers of the body and a curser of mankind (Psalm 59:1-8). The words, feelings, and attitudes that we exhibit towards others, good or bad, will either join us with Christ, or they will separate us. Only love will help the Father's will, as well as help ourselves. Anything less is helping Satan manifest in people's lives through our curses (Matt. 5:44).

Accuser really means...to curse.

To Curse or to Bless...
Jesus depends on our choice.

23

Probably the best book ever written on this subject is **Blessing or Curses by Derek Prince.** This is a *must read* for everyone!

Jesus said that no man has greater love than when he lays down his life for his enemies; Jesus did, so we must also (John 15:13).

Angels Can't Bind

Some people say that we cannot bind Satan or his demons, because Michael the Archangel only said, "The Lord rebuke you," for Moses' body (Jude 9). The truth is that was all that Michael needed to do and **could do,** because *Satan had the authority he took from Adam.* Satan gained the authority over the earth when he deceived Adam. This authority was higher than the angel's, but less than God's. **Jesus took back our lost authority on earth** through His victory on the cross, and gave it back to mankind to rule and reign the Father's will upon the earth; as it was supposed to have been done in the first place. As we line up in agreement with the Word and the Father's will, then, and only then, do we work together to bind and to loose the powers of darkness. This sets the captives free and empowers angels to war in the airways. One day we will rule and reign with Christ in heaven over angels and nations (Rev. 2:26). We must rule down here before we can rule up there. This is the time to train, not the time to play. Children play, while the adults work.

*Now is the time to work...we have
been children long enough!*

OUCH!
I sense an Angry Spirit starting to manifest!

Self-Deliverance

Self-deliverance is very powerful. Just simply recognize what spirits are manifesting themselves in your life, and command them to leave you in Jesus' name. Some people find it more powerful by looking in the mirror, but it can be done anywhere and at anytime you sense their activity. When a spirit leaves your body, there will be a response. The most common is yawning with tears or coughing. If your stomach ever feels nauseous, then definitely keep on binding and rebuking the spirits. Why in the stomach? I am not sure, but they do manifest there, and it is possible to actually feel them move up towards the throat as if to burp, like gas. If you vomit, it will not be food, but green bile from the stomach. This sounds weird I know, but I didn't start it out this way, it just is! Go with the flow and please don't fight it. It's not painful at all. As a matter of fact, once you feel the relief and freedom of things leaving, *you will not be satisfied until everything leaves.* The Holy Spirit will make a believer out of you if you only give Him half a chance. Sometimes believing must come through seeing, so let the anointing open your eyes for the seeing. If doubt, fear, or unbelief won't let you believe what I say here as being true, then there is a test. **The test is this:** *Start praising the Lord in sincere worship right now,* or wait until the next time you're in serious worship at church; and notice how often you yawn during that exact time. You know you are not sleepy during real worship, even if later on you are during the preaching...ha! Why do you think it feels good to worship the Lord? It is because the anointing is delivering you from stuff that you are not even aware of. Worship is more for us, than it is to puff up God. He doesn't need it, we do! That is why He says to praise Him in all things. Praise not only frees us, but it protects us from opening up doors for attacks. *There is nothing more powerful* you can do in your spiritual walk than to *praise the Lord in all things.* Simply ask the Holy Spirit to prove the validity of this truth and He will, if only we ask.

Even self-deliverance is not a one-time cure-all. Spirits will always be trying to get back in their self-proclaimed temple. If you get hungry, you simply eat something. If you sense evil trying to get a foothold in you, simply bind and rebuke it. It's no big deal! Just do it! It's more trouble to swat at the flies that harass us than it is to let them lay their eggs in our hair and minds; but in order to live healthy, we must eat properly; and so to live freer in the Spirit realm, we must swat properly. **Freedom must be fought for...the violent take it by force. Fight the good fight!**

Never, never, n.e.v.e.r. give up! The Host of Heaven is watching us, and counting on our true hearts and our tough jaws to run the race set before us.

Victory is not of ourselves, but by the grace of God. His grace is His ability of strength and power in us, to accomplish His purposes. Our part is to pray for, depend on, and accept His commission willingly, in a forward march to bring about His ultimate purposes. Simply put...*He is the power, but we pull the trigger.* His power and ability is available, but He needs us to point the gun barrels at His designated targets, and pull the triggers.

Videotapes Available

Note here: I produced a video that you can watch, and actually get deliverance, while at the same time learning how to do deliverance on others. It is so powerful that I guarantee it to make a difference in your life, or you get your money back...no questions asked. **Warning: Do not watch while driving...ha! ha!** Seriously though, we do have an audiotape of the same video that should not be listened to while driving. Deliverance is real stuff. *Blessed are those who fear not, and enter in.*

Once again... many people get deliverance during worship and do not even know it, even though they feel freer afterwards. I've experienced and seen many others yawning big time yawns, while in the very midst of all-out, hands-lifted-up worship. The very thought of being sleepy during joyful worship is just a silly lie from the enemy. You will experience this yawning the next time you enter into worship, wait and see for yourself. I have started having these big deep yawns by just coming into the presence of the Holy Spirit that was on a person or in a room. If you even talk about the Holy Spirit and deliverance, spirits will leave you. People around you will say, "Oh, I'm sleepy," but you will know better. Once you see and understand that demons flee your presence when the presence of the Holy Spirit is around you, all your fears will also leave. **Fear is only a demon** anyway, so get rid of it, and feel free to live life more abundantly. **No weapon formed against us can prosper...if...we steadily rebuke it.** I am even yawning at this very moment of typing this, and you probably are as well. What is it that is leaving me, you ask? I don't know for sure, and it doesn't matter to me as long as it leaves. It could be an assignment sent out against me to stop me from typing this; maybe sickness, depression, failure, distractions, frustration, laziness, or just something wanting to steal, kill, or destroy the Father's will in my life. Demons are even sent out on assignments to destroy us down the road in life. There is absolutely nothing to fear for yourselves, or for your loved ones when doing deliverance. Fear will tell you differently though, it's scared, but **whom do you listen to, fear or the Holy Spirit?** The Holy Spirit will never use fear or any other demonic trait to direct us in His will.

Spirit of Spleen

I once heard a demon speak out of a Spirit-filled woman's mouth, and confess that it was called spleen. When asked why it was there...since her spleen seemed to be okay at the time; it said it was sent to cause her spleen failure in the future. The spirit of spleen was bound, rebuked, and commanded to leave her in Jesus' name...and it did, as she coughed and coughed before regaining her composure and awareness of what had just happened. I put a few sessions on **videotape** because I knew the people would not believe it later, and this spleen spirit is just one of them. The special thing about doing deliverance or going through it, is that it brings instant hope for the future with joy, and peace in the present. It feels similar to the feeling of being born again. It is that freedom and joy that we all felt when Jesus first came into our hearts. I remember how joy poured in, as tears flowed out, as I exchanged, confessed and repented sins, for the forgiveness and love of Jesus' presence. I did not understand fully what was taking place then, but deliverance was happening, and it still is today. *Praise God forevermore!* If getting free was a one-time experience, then why do so many people backslide? It is because of the warfare going on over you and me. Even though Satan may have lost our souls to Jesus' Blood; Satan will constantly torment us with hindrances, that try to keep us ineffective in loosing other lost souls. When we put on the goggles of not just virtual reality, but true spiritual reality, then and only then, will we see as born-again believers. **We are the hope of Christ for lost souls,** and the bottleneck of difficulties for Satan's plans. There are three things that hold us back from helping Jesus bind and loose the enemy: unbelief, fear, and selfishness; no, there's four...

Indifference!

How can we say we love God whom we have not seen, and be so **indifferent** towards those He died for?

Hmmm...??? & ???...GO FIGURE!

We do not have to carry the whole world on our shoulders, just the world that evolves around us. This is our part of carrying our crosses. Our cross is not a burden too heavy for us. Jesus will not put upon us more than we can bear. We are to hold up the arms of the weak, the poor, the hungry, the lame, and the blind, deaf and dumb, in warfare intercession for the power of God to fill them with life and life more abundantly. We must snorkel down into the muck and the mire of satanic deception and grab onto the deceived, and hold their heads up above these cesspools long enough for the Light of Christ to fill them. Jesus came to rescue mankind; do we hinder His causes because we are content with our own salvation? **No!** If we are not helping Him, then we are hurting Him. We need the red badge of courage to carry the **Red Cross of Hope** into the battle of tides that are sweeping the helpless into the seas of despair and hopelessness. Are we going to be fighters on the beaches and shores of God's purposes, or just soak up the Son and flounder in shallow waters? Greater is He that is in us. Then let Him outside of our puny selves, and let the Creator of the Universe create in us a new thing, a good thing, a wonderful thing that is far above and beyond our imaginations. Let God be God, and get out of the way of saying, **"NO,** I don't feel like it," or "it doesn't bear witness to me." Humbug, that is just a self-centered, self-pity spirit, trying to convince you of having *its own way* in your life. Judge your thoughts and reactions to all this stuff. Would the Holy Spirit speak to you and cause those kinds of feelings to manifest in order to keep you from going forward?...Of course not! The enemy does not want you to get free, because you will set others free as well. I have seen it, heard it, and even videotaped it. When **demons** are asked why we are here, they **say, "You're here to cast us out." They say this about every believer that gets in their face.** They know far more than we do, that is why they hate us so much. There are no free rides in Christ. Once the enemy knows you belong to Christ, the battle heats up.

Fighting is a part of life no matter who we are. We will fight a life of constant defensive action and take little ground, or we can wake up to the fact that we are on the offensive side, and start taking back stolen ground, time, and lives that have been stolen from us all.

Cockle doodle do...it is later than we think... W.A.K.E....U.P.!

CHAPTER 4

Soul-Ties... "Good and Bad"

Jesus' Blood breaks soul-ties

What is of greater power than the Blood of Jesus? *Nothing!* Then place the Blood of Jesus between all relationships as a force field to protect or to preserve. **A soul-tie can be anything...person, place or thing that we have joined ourselves with in the past, or even in the present.**

Second John 1:10-11, TLB, says, **"If anyone comes to teach you, and he doesn't believe what Christ taught, don't even invite him into your home. Don't encourage him in any way. If you do you will be a partner with him in his wickedness."**

A soul-tie can even be just agreeing with someone about something. Agreement is joining yourself with it. A winking of the eye, and a nodding of the head and heart is saying, **"It's okay."** Joining oneself with a prostitute is a union of agreement, a oneness, a togetherness, a partnership, a compromise, and an ax blow to the tree of life within you. Any kind of winking at sin is an encouragement for it to continue on. Our association with it gives it life, and our abstention and rebuke gives it death. We are to be life givers by stomping on and choking out those seeds of unrighteousness that try to grow up among us through our agreement of winking the eye. Whether it is false religions, or agreement with sin...**by not saying, "No!" we say, "YES!"**

Phinehas' Righteous Anger

In **Numbers 25:1-17,** Israel was going down the tubes in sin through their adulterous actions with the Moabite girls. However, Phinehas finally had enough of their sins that brought God's wrath and plagues upon the people. In **verses 7-8,** he jumped up in righteous anger with his spear (a symbol of power in words) and ran into the tent of wickedness, and thrust his spear through the bodies of both the man and the woman. **We must get the point here...one way or the other!** His righteous anger stopped God's wrath. That my friend, is what God is looking for, people who will not compromise, nor tolerate sin any longer. Today, we do not war against the flesh and blood as Phinehas did, but we are to pierce the darkness through and through with deathblows of righteous anger.

Once again, a soul-tie is winking at, or agreeing with, thus encouraging it to live, by our not commanding it to die.

Soul-ties can be good, as well as bad.

We are in soul-tie with the Father, the Son, and the Holy Spirit, and with our brothers and sisters whom we agree with. Where two or more are gathered together in my name, there I AM in their midst, and let it be established. Beware of what you agree with, because you are becoming a partner with it, and will reap the fruit of it...good or bad. That is part of, **"lay not your hands on someone too quickly"** (1 Tim. 5:22).

Apply the Blood of Jesus

It's always better to be safe than sorry, so speak Jesus' Blood over all situations that rise up in front of you. The power in the Blood of Jesus is the wedge that splits soul-ties apart, or keeps them together. His Blood not only saves our souls from hell, but it is a wall of protection from the enemy devices. I have had demons tell me during deliverance sessions, who has the Blood applied to their lives. They do not say Blood, but call it that **red stuff;** just like they don't say Jesus, but say Him or "that guy." Anytime you are not sure if a demon is telling the truth, just ask them if that statement will stand true on judgment day. **They always back down if it is a lie.** There is not anything wrong with interrogating these demons for more insight as to *who else* is in the person; as long as it does not get into fortune-telling. After all, *we can* interrogate these enemies for information just like in the natural wars of battle. If this statement bothers you, then just cast it aside and go on, don't throw out the baby with the bath water. Several times while doing deliverance with people (believers only), I've had demons tell me they see the red stuff on my hands, as I wave them in their faces, and command them to see the Blood of Jesus, and be tormented by it. The first time I explained deliverance to a church body, I demonstrated how I wave my hands at the person, and command the demons to see it. Many people later came up to me, and

If they lie - how can one interrogate to gain insight?

30

said they felt something rise up inside them with contempt towards my actions. That made believers out of them, that something other than the Holy Spirit was living inside them. I was explaining it to a dear brother and friend one time in a restaurant, and he sat back quickly as I waved my hands and spoke of the Blood. He finally became a believer that demons can live in a Spirit-filled believer.

The Blood of Jesus must be called upon, imparted, and placed between any and all situations that can be used by the enemy as getting a foothold into someone's life. His Blood will keep the evil powers of unholy relationships, business deals, teachings, doctrines, and life changes at bay, like a barrier, or hedge of protection, as well as being the power to separate unholy ties, or protect good ones now in action. After binding these demonic powers with His Holy Blood, I believe we can call in from the North, South, East, and West, the blessed relationships and soul-ties that are ordained for us and others to have. If Satan can't get us tangled up into sin, then he will cause relationships of things or people, to just keep us distracted from the Father's will. **Distractions that cause delay, are still the same as not doing it, so Satan wins either way.** Wake up and look around, there are far more distractions today, than there were in the days of Jesus' earthly walk. Do we take any of these things with us when we leave this world? Will they be waiting for us in Heaven to play with...I don't think so! **Then why all the hustle and bustle for futility...maybe self-worth and accomplishment...say Amen or oh me!** Do you know what will be waiting for us there, for all eternity? Of course you do...the rewards of faithful obedience of prayers and helps, for the lost and dying souls all around us. Will the Lord say, "Well done," and parade our things before us? No! But **He will parade the lives of those who we helped get snatched from hell,** that decorate His crown. We sure don't want to get to the end of our lives and look back with regret at the little things that we could have done in order to make a difference in just one more life...like in the story of *Schindler's List.*

In the movie classic, *It's a Wonderful Life,* it may look like our mundane lifestyles, but we are not an accident in time, culture, sexual species, or even the exact moment we stand in right now. We are called for this exact day and hour to make a difference in our place and position. The Lord went through a lot of trouble to get us into these positions, for His purposes. Just like in that classic movie, we also effect all those around us, and *that, my friend...is the very reason for your next breath.* Effect those around you by binding the powers that hinder belief in Christ, while at the same time, loosing the Holy Spirit into their lives for their eternal glory. **The Father's high hopes are that none shall perish** (2 Peter 3:9).

I'm Not Called

You say, "I'm not called to evangelize," does this mean that you are not supposed to tell others about the saving power of the cross? If you freely receive...then freely give! How about intercession? What do you mean you're not called to intercede for others? Then give your tithes and offerings to help others fulfill their callings to teach and preach the Gospel truths. What do you mean, you don't have to give? Well, then bind and lose the powers of darkness so that the angels, the Holy Spirit, and His Word can be performed in people's lives! Not called to that either, hey? Well, praise God! I'm sure glad that the apostles didn't have this same attitude. If you have this do-nothing attitude, believe it or not, there is still hope for you. Simply get someone to do this 40-Day Warfare Plan, and put your name on their list. After 40 days, *you will* get newfound freedom to enter into your high calling as well. Try it, you have nothing to lose, but *all to gain.*

This may sound harsh, but a little slap in the face now is better then turning into one of the foolish virgins that never got into heaven because of their indifference and lack of preparation.

(I am really a nice guy! Blame this harsh stuff on the Lord! He has been stepping on my toes so much, that I act and look like a dancer in the streets of Laredo with a six gun shooting at my feet.)

The warfare going on over lost souls is very serious. It is the most important focus of heaven's witnesses. If it's the Father's will that none should perish, then it better become serious to us as well.

Prayer

Father,

We ask You right now to impart into us Your anointing of love and concern for the lost souls around us. Free us from all distractions that hinder us, so that we may fulfill the work that Jesus started. Let us carry the torch of Your love and Word into the enemy camps, and command the powers of darkness to see the Light of Christ and free their victims. Prove Yourself strong in our weak and frail temples. Your power must manifest itself through us in order to become useful in this last day's harvest. Give us insight of vision into Your causes and thrust us into the eye of the serpent with Your piercing sWORD of victory. Breathe new life into our temples with the fire of Your Holy Spirit, and strike down the enemy giants who trespass in the land of Your people's lives. Stand up in us, O Lord, with righteous anger, and proclaim Your greatness, Your power, and Your might over all the things that raise up their heads

in rebellion against Your perfect will in our lives, and in the lives of those around us.

O Lord, You are greater in us, than he that is in this world. Breathe upon our dry bones, and put new sinew upon our frames. Make us stand up and run towards the enemy like David did...with FAITH, and not fear.

Yes, and Amen!

CALL THEM AS YOU SEE THEM!

In the beginning of doing this warfare plan, I didn't know some of the names of the spirits that I saw operating in people's lives, so I just called them by what I saw them doing (which is still okay to do). I saw a fellow brother constantly bragging on people to their faces, yet belittling them behind their backs. Upon confronting him on this, he just said, "It was all in fun, some of the guys at work made an art of it." Well, I saw it as a kiss-up spirit, but I called it a brown nose spirit. After two weeks of he and this spirit being on my list, that I called out each day; he punched a guy at work in the face...that he normally had victory over. Well, he lost his job over that punch, but he hasn't manifested in that same spirit since then. I didn't know that he would lose his job, but I did know that he had to get free from that spirit. **I have been told that a brown nose would better be called a political spirit.** I never told this guy about my list in any way, and he still doesn't know it, unless he reads this book.

I put actors' names on my list that come to my mind as well as many different key figures in this world's society. They need help through our prayers. It doesn't matter who it is or what spirit seems to be manifesting in their life. It can be changed through warfare intercession.

Children Need Deliverance Too...

One time while doing deliverance with a couple that was taking several hours *(which it can very easily)*, their nine- and seven-year-old daughters came into the room. While they sat on the floor next to me, the seven year old sneezed. Her mother said that she had a cold or something like an allergy. Well, I just leaned back in my chair towards her and waved my hand over her, commanding that sickness to come out in Jesus' name. She started coughing and spitting up some green stuff in a waste-basket, and then sighed with relief. Her mother then said that ever since they were very little, they always fought each other when playing. I started binding and loosing spirits of anger, frustration, hatred, jealousy, and other spirits that hindered them from getting along. They both sat there coughing and spitting up this same green stuff for about 25 minutes. It was amazing to see this happening, because these children had no idea what we were looking for as far as reactions. The next day when the father came back for his part of deliverance, his wife told us that amazingly, the children played together peacefully all day for the first time. The little girls even came up to us and thanked us for helping them. A footnote on the father's session was that he wanted deliverance so bad, that he fasted all day. It was amazing how quick and easy the demons manifested and left him. The more desperate a person is, the more authority there is to make them leave. ***The determination of the will is a major factor for the authority of demonic eviction.***

The only reason for sharing this with you is not for any at-a-boys, but to help you believe in the necessity of deliverance in children, as well as in adults, that are the victims of generational curses. One thing is for sure, when it comes to deliverance, nobody is special. It does not take any special anointing or impartation to bind and loose demons from people's lives.

It's Not a Special Gift...It's a Command!

We are all commanded to cast out demons and set the captives free. The only ones who are not doing it are either uninformed, fearful, or just don't care.

Once informed, you will care, and by doing it, all your fears will leave.

Flesh or Demons...Both!

I say both, because demons weave themselves into our beings to the point of becoming as one. At birth, we had very small wills, yet generational curses from parents and relatives before us, opened up doors for demonic attributes of will and actions to start inflicting us. As a baby, *the number one spirit, selfishness,* started manifesting itself in us. And as we grow up, we continue to gather and manifest spirits that were contrary to the Father's will, and our parents. That is why psychologists always go back to our childhood when tracing problems; looking for open doors into children's lives from their relatives. **Self-centeredness becomes the dominant will of our flesh.** When our wills agree with spirits of selfishness, then they (the spirits) become a part of us, our flesh. When we recognize these spirits are trying to impose themselves upon us, we can then rebuke them from our wills...our flesh. **It is our agreement with them that gives them life. We have the choice to either give them life or death. *Choose right!*** When Jesus saved our souls, upon our being born again, He also delivered us from many spirits that were at war against the Holy Spirit's will. As we agree with the Holy Spirit's will, then the flesh dies, and we become more Christlike. Our wills are the same as our decisions. We get a thought or a feeling that tries to sway our decision of wills in certain directions of action. The fruit from these actions determine the degree of light or darkness within us. **Selfishness is the hub of flesh,** with many other demonic traits attaching themselves like spokes on a wheel. *Selfishness is their lifeline to operate their wills into our wills, while manifesting themselves into becoming THEY themselves, instead of us.* That is why most people do not even know who they really are. It is because demons have convinced the person that it is just their fleshly make-up of personality and not demons themselves. That is why the Lord can forgive us so easily when we repent, because He sees us as the victims that we really are. We were made to be lions that would rule and reign with the roaring Word of God within us, but we are infected with so many demonic thorns that we mostly go around like a pussy cat being kicked around from pillar to post. It's time to **roar,** and **roar,** and **roar some more,** by pulling out these demonic thorns from ourselves as well as from each other.

Even baboons have enough sense to pick fleas from each other; surely we can be as smart!

Simply put, you are in the flesh to the degree that you give your wills over to demonic temptations, **which allows them to use your temple for their purposes, *not yours, nor the Holy Spirit's.***

Our judgment will depend upon the degree in which we allow demons to manifest through us...*when we know better.*

Our Selfishness vs. Our Selflessness

Darkness vs. Light.
Satan vs. God.
Our Flesh vs. the Holy Spirit.

There is ground to be lost or gained, which will be rewarded down here, as well as up there!

They can be stolen or protected...you choose.

So next time you say, "Oh, the devil made me do it," know that he didn't without your help. Judgment day for us all will be determined on how much we helped the causes of Satan vs. God, through our submission or rebellion to the will of the Father, the Son, and the Holy Ghost. *Determine to will right, and live right,* thus saving time in the long line on Judgment Day, so that we can all get on with the Big Dinner Party ...Hurray! Hurray! Praise Jesus!

You see, the truth that I have been trying to point out of what is really happening to every living soul breathing today, as well as to those on their way, is that **demonic powers are trying to continually live out their purposes in people's lives, and we don't even know it.** Perishing for lack of knowledge is a fact of life, because of our lack of knowledge, and our strength of wills. It's the job of those who say they see; to break these trespassers back from the innocent, long enough for the Holy Spirit to strengthen their wills. So they can say, "In Jesus' name, no more will you rule this temple for your own pleasures, I bind and rebuke you, in Jesus' Name!"

We will then be helping the Father, the Son, the Holy Ghost, the Word, the angels, the people, and the earth, through our joint union of binding and loosing demonic powers. We do not live as unto ourselves only, but pass on blessings or curses, as vessels of heritage for both good and evil. Through our obedience of continually breaking the powers of generational curses, we create generational blessings that will be passed down to future generations. We will be helping the causes of Christ, by hindering darkness from entering through legal doorways of generational curses. Now we can see why Jesus said that we are either helping Him...or hurting Him. Knowing the truth will set you free, yet at the same time, *truth makes you responsible and liable* (Luke 12:48). The reason why Christ was sinless, was because He obeyed His Father's will in His decisions of will, and *lived selfless*.

They Mirror Their Feelings

Oftentimes a demon will mirror its feelings within its victim by making them feel their same feelings, and convincing *their* **person** that they are feeling the spirit of the place or person in which they just came into contact with. Demons will further try to convince the person that it is the Spirit of God witnessing within them, through the revelation that this situation is not of God. Even though the Holy Spirit does reveal truth to us about a place or thing, He does it to help fight those forces...not run away in fear or contempt. The Lord wants to help...not cast aside. Religious spirits react the same today as they did in Jesus' Day, through the Religious Pharisee Spirit.

An example:

I remember one time when a teacher was teaching on deliverance one night, and was going to do it for anyone interested the next night. His teaching was right on with sound teaching and Scriptures about the fact that believers needed deliverance. The next day a girl came to me all upset and frustrated as to why he had taught those things. She said she didn't feel in her spirit that he was right. I asked her if she was sure that she was listening to the **Right Spirit,** and she angrily replied back, that she knew how to hear the Holy Spirit. The point is: Demons will manifest their own fears by convincing their person through fears, doubt, worry, suspicion, uneasiness, anxiety, etc., etc., that they are correct in hearing God's voice as being warned away from these falsehoods, even though they can clearly see that God's hand of love and mercy is moving in supernatural ways. Doesn't this sound like Jesus and the Pharisees? The Holy Spirit **does** give us the gift of discernment to warn us from falsehood and temptations, but **He does not use fear as a tactic** to hinder us from getting freer and closer to Jesus. The Holy Spirit's whole motive for living in us is to edify our minds, our bodies, and our souls into a closer walk with Jesus; while at the same time, to help needy souls around us. When a thought or feeling comes over you with doubt, suspicion, or fear, stop a moment and ask yourself these questions: "Would the Holy Spirit make me think and feel this way? What would be His motives for this? Do these emotions stir up love, or criticism? Do I feel hopeful or hopeless? Does it edify and enlighten my soul, or smother it with confusion? What is the fruit that grows on this situation?" These are real questions, for real answers, to real problems. Even little choices of wrong discernment in hearing the Holy Spirit, can and will hinder us from ever getting as free as the Father wills for us. One major question that brings instant clarity to whether or not it is the Holy Spirit, or another spirit is this: *"Is my response selfish and self-centered, or is it selfless and giving?"* Only those who truly want to follow the Lord in all **His Ways** will ask these questions. Why? Because the enemy will bombard us with the same old justifiable reasons, as to why we do not have to give in. To the degree in which we die to self or selfishness, is the degree in which the Father can use us. Satan tempted Jesus in the wilderness to be selfish, but Jesus, once again, dying to self, won the victory for more dependant power from the Father. Our thoughts and feelings must be discerned properly in order for us to become led along properly. Failure to gird up the loins of our minds when we know better will be revealed as rebellion or pride, which the Lord will resist. Let us now resist the powers of darkness, with all their wicked devices of deceit and selfishness; no longer surrendering our wills over to their justifiable reasoning of excuses. We must pick up our crosses, our shields of faith, and the Sword of the Word within us. Let us crucify the enemy of our minds, and take back the stolen land of our wills and our blessings. I use to think, "What land must I take back?" Then I realized that God's will for me and for others, that we call blessings, are being hindered and stolen by the devil through our own wrong choices of hearing and following the Lord's leading. It is not just the blessings of good things that we receive from the Lord, but we become coworkers with His very purpose on earth. His purposes are far and away of greater importance than our meager comforts and pleasures in this life, but we are deceived into believing that He only exists for our own puny selves like a genie in a lamp. It is time to put away the foolishness of spoiled children and fight the good fight of faith, while ushering in the Lord's return.

Little Spirits in Heaven

I have a personal belief that has not hindered my walk, but on the contrary, it helps me grasp insight into the bigger picture of God's purposes through us. I cannot prove it and it does not really matter if it's true or not, but if I'm wrong, it will not matter when I reach Heaven anyway. I've been advised not to put this in the book. They say that it takes away from the message of warfare intercession. But on the contrary, I think that it has purpose of greater understanding as to why we are here, and what should be our attitude.

I heard a popular evangelist tell about his visitation to heaven, and he explained that he saw little spirits flying around in heaven saying, "Send me to earth, I want to be a living soul, send me!" That just confirmed my own feelings that we were spirits in heaven before we came into our bodies on earth, just like Jesus was in heaven before He came to earth in His. Whether or not this is true does not really matter. The point is this: I just imagine that these millions of little spirits are crying out for the Father to send them to earth so they can proclaim God's goodness on earth, as well as becoming a part of His greater eternal purposes. I can just imagine the Father saying, "Look here, you little spirits, you can see how difficult it is to live in a human. They are constantly in a warfare struggle against sin and the great deceiver; and there is no guarantee that you will be a born-again soul...you may end up in hell." I can hear them reply, "It's worth the chance! We know that Your mercies are everlasting, and You are slow to get angry.

"We want the chance to praise Your Holy name on earth as we now do in Heaven. We want to take the chance that You will keep us in all our ways, for we know that You will never forsake those who follow You. The opportunity to sit with You for all eternity is the highest honor of opportunity given to any living creature. We want this opportunity to rule and reign for Your good pleasures. Make us a human, a living soul, a helper, and a soul mate for You...P.L.E.A.S.E.!"

"Okay, fine, but you know that in order to win your souls in this race of life, you will have to trust Jesus, My Word, the Holy Spirit, and praise Me in all things; and love unconditionally those who are not lovable. If you are one of the chosen few, you will have to proclaim My Word with boldness, free from the fear of man...lay hands on the sick and pray for their healing...and casting out demons is part of proclaiming My power of love and forgiveness. Many will hate and persecute you for My name-sake. You will be betrayed, tortured, and killed in many diabolical ways, but I will be there to bring you home...*if you stay faithful.* No matter what happens, **faithful-**

ness is y.o.u.r. part of My plans...I'll do the rest." "Okay, Lord, that seems only fair to us. Your yoke is made easy, and Your burdens are light. All things are made possible for those who believe. **Can we go now?"**

The point of this story is not to throw anyone offtrack about this book's purpose, but to make us think about the bigger picture. What if we each said we would proclaim His purposes on earth as Jesus did. If so, then we should wake up and smell the coffee and fulfill our very reason for existence. These little spirits had to be dependent on the love of God, but also on the prayers of the everyday believer to pray them through.

I believe that we, as born-again believers, who say we see, are by-products of the chain reaction prayers of those who did see clearly before us, and prayed us in. ***Now, it is our free will choice,*** as to whether or not we will be thankful for just our own salvation and go along our merry ways of indifference, or will we be thankful enough to those who prayed us in, and **pray this blessing onto those who think they see, but are really...BLIND INDEED.**

Will someone help the blind?

WE WANT TO SEE TOO!
P L E A S E...

CHAPTER 5

Warfare Prayer, Taking Ground From the Enemy, Setting the Captives Free

Warfare is fighting, not with flesh and blood, but against the powers of darkness in the airways all around us that blind and hinder people from seeing and believing the Gospel, and reaching out for freedom in Christ. Loved ones, friends, neighbors, even our enemies, as well as ourselves, are all caught up into a tangle of powers between our Savior and the destroyer. Our struggle to serve Jesus is often hindered by satanic forces that try to choke us from becoming effective in helping others believe the love and salvation power of Jesus (Luke 8:14).

Everyday we struggle to keep ourselves from becoming ensnared again with demonic tricks, that continually lay a net out before us to trip us, and then condemn us as failures and worthless Christians. Jesus said we are more than conquerors because we are in Christ Jesus, but do we really feel it and believe it? Most of the time we don't! Yet we can sometimes feel paroled or pardoned on Sunday morning services as the presence of the Holy Spirit holds off the accusing powers for a time, so that we can once again feel free and alive. It is then that guilt and condemnation from the accuser is held back so that we can feel remorse, and repent of sins and failures, and then receive, believe and feel the Lord's forgiveness. Mostly it is us forgiving ourselves which is our biggest problem and Satan's biggest tool.

The warfare prayer of binding and loosing of demonic powers from our world is mandatory in becoming effective soldiers for Christ. His power is ready and waiting to be released against evil powers, but it must be sent, called upon, claimed, and released by our faith through warfare prayer. Bombarding the powers of darkness that hang over the people placed in our world with the powers of light, will cause darkness to fall down piece by piece, demon by demon, until those blind to Christ and asleep to His love, will awaken and hear, see, feel, and understand all that Christ has done for them. If we are real soldiers, then after we have enlisted into His service, gone through His boot camp, become equipped and empowered to fight the good fight and to do His works, we will fulfill our callings—our enlistment—our work—our duty—our job—and His will. "Well done, thou good and faithful servant," is **then** said to us. How will we fulfill this call of a soldier, a servant, a bondservant, a hired hand, a faithful child, a partner with Christ, a helpmate? However we see ourselves in Christ, it is our call as soldiers-in-arms to pick up His weapons and our cross, and go into all the world and fight the good fight to set the captives free. Freedom is Christ's goal for mankind...it must be ours as well!

He Sent Us!

All the world can be reached if we each fight for the world that evolves around us. We each have our own world to conquer first, before taking on other ground. We are solely responsible for our kingdom just like David was over his. Our Father placed David in a position to help His people, to protect them from the enemy, to encourage them into a deeper commitment with the Lord, to lead them to victory, and to enjoy the spoils of their battles and the fruit of their labors.

Peace was David's goal, but battles fought for deliverance from the enemy was the first priority before peace could come. Evil must be cast off and out, before peace can enter. The moneychangers must be cast out with a righteous anger first, then the people can worship in peace and holiness.

We too are placed as kings to reign over the kingdoms set before us. Our personal world or kingdom is scattered all around us like a flock of sheep. The wolves are stealing, killing, and destroying the sheep all around us, while we sit and play our flutes. There is a time to flute and a time to fight. Knowing the difference is accomplished by walking in the Spirit. When we are led by the Spirit, we will fight and flute in the Spirit. To do only one is failure, because both are required. David knew the difference, Jesus did, and so must we.

Blood is required of us. To whom much is given, much is required. The blood of Jesus protects us and empowers us to cause a blood spill in the airways where darkness rages against the innocent victims around us. Jesus bruised the head of Satan like David did Goliath, but He commissioned us to cut off his head, not literally, but spiritually, and to stand upon his corpse and proclaim victory for the innocent, and to defeat the enemy troops.

We are more than conquerors, but we don't feel it, so we don't believe it. It was said about us from Him who sees and understands all things. Yet, we belittle His insight because we cannot see it for ourselves. You see...we are blind! Blind to the truth, so we grope around looking for someone to lead us by the hand. Blind hands only get stepped on and bitten by things that lurk in darkness, waiting for our reaching out instead of our reaching up. Our Lord only takes our hands when they reach upward like a child being held as it takes its first steps across a room. Even though He wants us to be and stay child-like, because it keeps us humble and dependent on His power and strength, He demands that we be warriors...righteously angered soldiers of war against the demonic powers of the airwaves. We are to fear nothing that the enemy tries or claims he can do. We are the winners. We are related to the Key Holder, the Victorious One, the Overcomer. David warred against flesh and blood, but we are not supposed too, yet some Christians seem intent on killing their wounded and discouraging new recruits.

Our enemy is not at eye level or arms length, but at artillery level. We have the power to fill the airwaves with enough artillery fire to bring down all the demonic planes that circle around our households and the flock of those in our world that God holds us accountable for. He would not say "Well done," if there was not something to be done! Five can take down 100, and 100 can take down 10,000 (Lev. 26:8). **JOSHUA 23:10** says, that one can chase 1000. Now that is power! Power that only God can provide and multiply, but He needs us to manifest His power. We are **enlightened** soldiers; no longer civilians of darkness that we once were. We have only been enlisted and enlightened, because of **His potential** through us. **We are called to be fighters, not whiners.** Fighters run toward the enemy and fight the good fight, while whiners sit and cry, "Why, Lord, why me, give me, give me..." hands out instead of hands up. Many are called, but few are chosen...He does not lie! He separates today just like in the days of old. His power is not for the multitude, but for a few good and faithful ones.

It is not enough for us to watch and hear a few Green Berets on television, radio, or in the pulpits spout the watchword call for today. We are Soldiers of Fortune...Eternal Fortune...Mercenaries for Christ! We have been bought with a price to do the work that the **Father called each of us to do.** We must say, *"NO"* to the darkness and *"YES"* to the light. It is time to stand up and be counted.

ENOUGH IS ENOUGH! Pick up your armor...put it on! Not Saul's armor, but the armor which fits your frame of mind and stature, so that you can run and not stumble. Pick your stones of the Word, hurl them at the enemy's forehead, and purge our God-given land (our world) from evil and darkness. We are to chase the enemy, and *never never turn our backs on them,* because our backs have no armor covering. Even though Jesus promises to cover our backsides, that is only from blind attacks, not from retreats. The victories in this Promise Land are for us to take by force. We are not to fear, but to forge across the rivers that separate us from His promises, while leading others across and casting out the enemies of God (the powers that rule in darkness). We only murmur and complain when we cannot see or understand why or what God is trying to do. When we fight against the darkness that surrounds us, we can then see more clearly in all things, with the mind of Christ.

Darkness is our enemy, not
those around us, or even ourselves.

The watchword call for today is...CHARGE!

"Who will stand up and say, 'Lord, I will volunteer to go and do all that You require of me for Your good pleasure and purpose...not my will be done, but Yours O Lord, my strength and my Redeemer.' "

The Commander's Orders Are...

(1) Know your sheep, the flock you shepherd over.
(2) Guard the names of those entrusted into your kingdom.
(3) Know your enemies...their strengths and their plans.
(4) Gather the powerful weapons made available to you for battle.
(5) Realize with understanding faith, the will and power of your Commander-in-arms.
(6) Most of all, stay on the horse that He placed you on. This is no time to fall off, because the enemy is being trampled under foot. Beware of playing around. Only the upright riders will keep their head...not all riders in general.

Heroes are earned, not born. Be found in the charge, not in the chastisement. Get up, stand up, and saddle up. Yell, "Charge!" **Scare the hell out of hell, and set the captives free to feast!** This is not a game to play, but a war to win! These are battles to be fought and won in the airways.

True King's Kids

Greater is He who is in us than he that is in the world (1 John 4:4). That is why David had the courage to fear not when the bear and lion stole away his Father's sheep. David ran and attacked the attacker by the jaw, and clubbed them into submission and even to death (1 Sam. 17:34-36). He set the captives free by being alert and ready in all seasons, shod with the preparation to help and overcome the enemies of the land. Goliath was no match for him after doing hand-to-hand combat with lions and bears. Satan's kingdom is no match for us either. His only power comes from those of us who give it to him through fear, worry, and lack of faith and knowledge. Satan's demons are under our David-like feet with their heads ready to be cut off. Swing the sword (the Word) of faith, and dismember death; giving life to those lives placed in our care. **David was an earthly king, as well as a spiritual king. We are only spiritual kings** to guard, protect, help, nurture with love, and honor others as being more important than ourselves. We are kings to guard, not to surrender over. Kings to fight, not to fumble. Kings to give, not to get as King's kids. Kings to love, not to lust for pleasure. Kings to overcome, not to whine, murmur and complain as spoiled children. God has no brats for long...fence straddlers, that is. King's kids have become nothing more than those who eat of the spoils they did not earn. They do not fight for anything, but they demand their own way above others. Their hands are always outstretched for more of what they can get for themselves. "Give me more Lord, so I can give away more." **"Ha!"** says the Lord. "Get off your backside and do the work set before you. No free rides here! No loafers or idle hands in My plans, rest only comes after the work, not before.

"The lazy and sluggard will I cast aside because he buries My investment in the ground, instead of multiplying an increase. That which he thinks he has will be taken and given away. To those who have much, to them more will be given."

Luke 12:48, Matt. 25:24-30

The battle is on! The waves are raging! Not waves of playing and surfing, but waves of unrest as the powers of the airways clash in battle for the souls of man. Satan is out to win over God's purposes, but God's purposes are for His men and women to overcome the waves of persecution and darkness. ***Nothing good ever comes easy,*** and it will not start today. We must work and labor with endurance and be persistent with steadfast running into the jaws of satanic forces with the club (the Sword) dipped in the blood of Jesus. This is His battle plan for us today. Take back, take back, and take back all that has been stolen by the thief and his accomplices.

The rope is taut across the chasm that separates heaven from hell in people's lives today. We are to pull with all our might in Christ in this **GREAT TUG-OF-WAR.** There must be more of us than there are with them. Don't you see, we can win, if we only pull and pull some more until death do we part from our part, during our short time on earth. Heavenly cheers go up for those who pull until the end, without letting their oil run out. With the oil we stay lubricated and mobile, able to do the work set before us. **Without the oil,** we start to squeak, murmur and complain, tire out, and rust up into complacency and compromise.

45

King David's greatest memories and pleasures to God were in his victories of battle, his going forward with hopes of overcoming and taking ground from his enemies. His greatest failures were in the midst of **idle time,** walking upon his house-top, counting his blessings instead of sticking to the battle plans of today's siege against the enemy fortress. *Idle time is not from God* unless it is a time of rest that follows His works. When you rest from His works, you will be **too tired to lust** for the flesh of life.

Satan Will Reward Your Idle Time

Man mostly wants to stay busy doing something, so Satan will busy your idle hands with distractions, or give you the impression that you are busy for God, but really for pride and self-righteousness.

Prov. 16:17

Prayer vs. Warfare

What is warfare...it's fighting! What is prayer...it's talking! We must talk to one and fight the other! Fighting is every bit a part of our nature as it is to talk and love. We are commanded to talk to our Father and love Him and His creation, while raising our fist against the same evil that He fights. He created us in His image, and fighting the real enemy instead of each other, is part of being like Christ in all things. **Our enemy is not at eye level,** it's at a level above us, yet below the throne of God. Demonic powers cannot rise anymore, so they descend upon us to take us down with them. They don't hate us as much as their hatred is first toward Jesus and His blood of redemptive power. We are the victims of their hate towards our Father. Their father of lies hates our Father of truth. It's not as personal as it may seem sometimes. Satan hates us because we have more authority than he does...when we use it! Greater is He that is in us! No matter how personal Satan tries to make it.

WE MUST MAKE IT MORE PERSONAL AGAINST HIM

Jesus made it personal by going to the cross, then taking away Satan's keys of death and hell. If we are to be counted worthy of sitting with Christ, then we must stay under the blood covering, and keep up the siege against spiritual powers, breaking down the walls of darkness!

Fighting is a fact of life. You will fight! If you don't fight in the airwaves around your flock, then the enemy will take ground closer to your home, and cause you to fight your families. When that ground is lost, then you will be in a self-survival battle day by day just to keep your head above being buried alive.

There is HOPE for the fighter but none for the fearful.

What did David or even Jesus receive, that was worth having without first a fight? Nothing! Nothing good and worthwhile! Solomon did though...big deal, Solomon! Now there is a King's kid that earned nothing by his battle scars! He just lavished upon himself all the blessings that his Father earned for him. He denied himself nothing at all. Since it was all given to him so freely, it meant nothing to him as worthwhile. **"All is futile,"** was his constant complaint. Did his Father have this same attitude? No, but King's kids of today do. How worthless and futile are spoiled kids that usually earn nothing for the kingdom and fall away in the end anyway, like Solomon did (1 Kings 11:4). A pearl of great price is fought for, dug for, and cherished forever. The silver platter is not of God while on earth, but it will be at the Great Supper. **Work first...eat later.** Don't work—don't eat! Isn't it only fair? Of course it is! His judgment is just. Jesus said the workers are few, the harvest is ripe, so pray for more help to do the reaping. We are called to be reapers, not owners of barns full of truth and deeper truths. **How fat do we need to get?** The pathway is narrow to the gate to Jesus. I don't believe that becoming **a spiritual fat-cat** will allow us to squeeze through His narrow gate. Satan doesn't care how fat we get, so long as we keep it in our barns of selfishness and spiritual pride. The Pharisees were so full of truth they could pop, but it did them no good at all, because they stumbled over their own fat and many never squeezed through the needle gate to heaven. If this offends you, then rebuke religious spirits, and your peace and joy will return again.

Our salvation is bought with Jesus' blood, but the **"Well done, thou good and faithful servant,"** is only said to those who keep on *doing the works* of the Father's will. Whether it is big or small, our work must be His work, if not, then it's as futile as Solomon's works.

The days of spiritual school and college play are past. Today is the day of "go ye forth," "do thy works," "the day is far spent," "stay alert," "do not be deceived," "count it all lost," "light your lamps," "shout it from the housetops," "shod your feet," "be ready in and out of season," "be ready to give an account," "fear not," "worry not," "press toward the mark of the high calling," "run your race," "fight the good fight," and "be not weary." Go! Go! Go! Go!

You say, **"how, where,** and **when?" Start today...**in your prayer closet...in full armor! The work that He has started in you, He will finish, but we must say, "Yes Lord, let's do it today and each day, until death do we part from this work of Your high calling."

We are suppose to be a David...not a Solomon.
Davids on earth...Solomons in heaven.

Don't get them confused! The Lord hasn't! You were chosen like David was to rule, to reign, to conquer, and to protect the Father's people, places, and things. You are like a king with all power in the heavenlies to conquer the enemies of the airways; taking the land for **the purpose of setting the captives free,** and ushering in the return of Christ Jesus.

You are only responsible for those people in your world that the Lord brings into your life, whether they are of blood, friends, neighbors, enemies, or even foreigners or acquaintances. They have entered your world for safekeeping by the Lord to protect and encourage.

David ruled over the physical make-up of man, but we are only to rule over his spiritual make-up. **Control not the body, but the powers over the body.** Binding and loosing is for and against the powers of darkness, not for controlling man himself. Man is a free will agent to decide and choose, but we the chosen by Christ are to bind the evil powers from man's mind and will, so that he can see clearly and make clear choices without deceptions. Evil is waging war against the mind of man to keep him in spiritual darkness. Man's only hope is that Jesus and His servants will counter-attack this enemy, and set him free in all fairness of choice. *The people placed in our world are unknowingly dependant on us to see further than they can,* and to break these powers off them. Jesus is depending on us too, and today is the beginning of the rest of our high calling.

It's never too late to begin warfare prayer.

How? Make a list of all the people that come to mind who make up your world: people at work, church, play, neighbors, relatives, acquaintances, etc. Every name of each family is not mandatory, because darkness can be broken off our bloodline and our spouse's bloodline back to ten generations above and below the person you listed. It will be best to get a notebook or tablet, because names will be added continually as the Lord trusts the faithful ones with more responsibility each day. Include your family and yourself on your people list, because they are under attack. Then focus on Satan's plans of deception, and how he attacks man through demonic attacks like depression, hatred, divorce, cursing, suicide, abortion, jealousy, lust, greed, confusion, guilt, condemnation, bad memories, nightmares, fears, worry, poverty, bitterness, unforgiveness, doubt, and unbelief, etc. The list goes on as you can see. Non-believers as well as Christians are bound by these demonic powers, and want to get free, but very often never really shake loose. If they do, it seems like they get caught up again. Victory is possible, but sometimes it takes more than just our own warfare to overcome these powers. That is why we need to war for each other as troops united in one mind. Five can take out 100, and 100 can take out 10,000, and more can be devastating (Lev. 26:8, Josh. 23:10). We can all be of one mind if we all focus on one goal...setting the captives free! The Father, Son, and Holy Spirit are one and the same, and all of our spirits can be one and the same with the same goal. Setting the captives free was what motivated Jesus to go on the cross. Freedom must be our goal for picking up our cross. It's easier than physical death, even though it will mean death to parts of our own will. **Death to self is a good thing.** Christ wants us dead to self, not just dying a little here and there. Death to self means Christ resurrected in us, through us, and for us, so that we might do His works, and even greater works by carrying His cross and setting the captives free. Just because we are saved doesn't mean we are totally free. Demon powers attack us so we will not shine for Christ and lead others out of bondage. They want us so down in failure, self-pity, depression, and other foul emotions, so that we will do what Job's wife said, "Curse God and die" (Job 2:9). Demons know that **we can hurt ourselves** more than they can. They can't pluck us from God's hand, but we can choose to leave it if we feel like God isn't good enough to us...**poor babies!** Satan lures us to complain our way out of God's protection and right into his rule of authority, with his free right to torment us, as we cause ourselves to be turned over for correction, because of rebellion to the Word.

Knowing our enemy's names and plans will help us to fight for those in our care. This is not the time to perish for lack of knowledge. Knowledge begets understanding, understanding begets authority, authority begets power, and power begets freedom from demonic powers that cause our self-will to become our idol. Most of us have made **an idol for ourselves,** not consciously but unconsciously, because of the king's kid syndrome...it lives in the mirror. Self is made an idol when it is the topic of our prayers. Our Father knows our needs before we pray and will actually answer our hearts desires when we pray for others as more important. The man that begged the storekeeper for a loaf of bread in the night was desiring it for his guest as more important than himself. Even though he benefited also, he wouldn't have sought that earnestly for himself, but for the hungry and innocent he did. That may be why the storekeeper gave in, not just because he was aggravated (Luke 11:5-8).

Our Heavenly Storekeeper will always come down and meet our heart's desire, if these desires are of His heart. Do you think the Good Samaritan did his own desire in helping the wounded man? Of course not! It was a costly and time-consuming experience. However, it probably wasn't the first time he did it since he seemed to do it so naturally. Could that be why he seemed to be wealthy, because he had done it before and God richly blessed him back? (Luke 10:30-38). Our Father promises to meet all our needs as we look around and focus our attention on the needs of others. The Holy way of getting is first giving. Jesus gave first, so must we also!

Good Samaritans—Good Soldiers, they are both the same.

What are we waiting for? The battle is raging all around us. Warring angels are posed ready for our directions for aerial attacks against the enemies of the air. We are to protect those who cannot protect themselves.

Spiritual warfare is the battle of the ages that we are enlisted into. Today is the day of salvation and enlistment. The fight is on, and it will not quit until the Day of Judgment when the Book is opened and the pit is filled. Oh, the agony of heaven as it groans for the soldiers of today. The harvest is great, but the workers are few (Matt. 9:37). Let us sign up today without waiting to be drafted. **Boot camp awaits the hearty of the high calling.** I have heard it said in a meeting, "We have enough power in this room to change the world." Then why don't we? **The Lord is ready!** Is there a higher calling than marching with Jesus and changing the world? Is there a second choice of greater importance? No! Jesus says, **"go-do-become empowered, charge-charge-charge!"**

Binding and loosing is the charge. The charge of today, and for all the tomorrows. Charge, fight, and war against the princes and powers of the air. Get mad! Yes, I said, "Get mad!" Jesus did. He had righteous anger toward the moneychangers, and so we have to get angry as well. Get mad at what is happening to our temple of the Holy Spirit and the temple of others. Jesus put His temple on the line as He fought for His Father's temple, where people could worship. We must fight in righteous anger against the powers that try to pollute the temples around us. As we fight for others, we will shake our own. Jesus whipped the physical, but we must whip the spiritual, and the physical will line up. Only then will the Holy Spirit shine out of our physical, and draw men into the spiritual, as they see Him working through us. Seeing is believing, but how can they see when satanic powers blind their eyes? Yelling at man to see only makes him more afraid and makes him turn away in fear. The blinders are the problem, and man himself is powerless to remove them. *All who claim to see...let them see.* Let them look around beyond the mirrors of self-awareness. See as the Spirit sees, as the Father sees, and even as the angels see. Oh ye of blind eyes, don't say you see unless you do. It is better for all of us to say, "O Lord, I'm blind to Your purposes. Anoint my eyes each day to see as You see, and move me by Your Spirit to war against the blinders on man. Fulfill Your will through me today." Let us fight the good fight and do all that our General commands.

HE BUILDS A TROOP...NOT A PLAYMATE!

Beelzebub...Lord of Flies

It has been said that Satan (Beelzebub) is lord of the flies. Did you know that when flies have to be exterminated from an area, that the area must be sprayed every day for 40 days to kill the new offspring that hatch out. Forty days of temptation with Jesus, or 40 years in the wilderness with Moses, is like 40 days of persistent disinfecting of an area that we wish to rid of Satan's infections. Satan is a short-term fighter. Scriptures tell how he had to leave Jesus for a time, after 40 days of temptation. The truth here is that if we can be faithful in waging war against Satan's kingdom for 40 days, he will have to leave for a time or a season as Scripture explains (Matt. 4:11, James 4:7).

The Birthing of the 40-Day Plan

Upon grasping this as revelation for a 40-day fight, I made a list. On July 24, 1993, I listed all the people of my world, saved and unsaved, friends and enemies, acquaintances and distant names. Another list was made up of demonic powers and their rank of authority. Once a day for six days a week, for 40 days, I bound out loud the names of these demon powers in order to break them off the people on my list, as well as their bloodline back to ten generations. On each seventh day (Sunday) I rested from binding demon powers, and called the people's names out loud for the Lord to loose them to see, hear, and obey His will for their lives. Then there was again six days of battle (Mon.-Sat.) binding and calling out loud the demons names only, and then resting from war (Sunday) and loosing the Holy Spirit upon the names of the innocent victims. If I missed a day, I would start over again with the 40 days since it should not be broken. During these 40 days, I would make a list of dated praise reports that came to me. It was amazing to see and hear how God moved when we gave Him binding and loosing to work with.

The Legal Realm

You see I believe there is some sort of legal realm that operates between God and Satan. Even though God is all-powerful, He still doesn't override our wills, and that my friend, is Satan's loophole. What we sow, we shall reap...that sounds like a law to me. It is this law of sowing that Satan depends on to have a legal right to reap havoc in our lives. Generational curses are real examples of legal rights where demons reign in freedom. Even though Jesus broke the curse of death and hell for us when He saved us, there are still tickets to pay for, the **red lights** run through from our past generation, that freely followed us down the line. Legal rights are legal, whether they are of God or Satan. Right is right, and fair is fair, because God is just. Adam and Eve sowed and we still reap today, now that is a generational curse for sure! Even though we are free from their curse, freedom must be claimed and fought for, or its effects still remain. Since God is just, He made an atonement for that curse with Jesus' blood, so that **today we can sow and reap generational blessings.** *That is the law and it will be judged.*

Choose ye this day, blessings or curses, but beware, we will reap what we sow and fall to the right for God, or to the left for demonic attacks. These attacks do not mean we are unsaved, it just means that we have to clean up our field in these areas. Can strife get into a marriage without someone sowing and opening the door? Of course not! Satan tricks us like he did Eve and then Adam. What about the innocent sheep of our flocks that don't even know the truth or don't want to? They will perish for lack of knowledge. *Let you who are strong, try to lead back the lost and wounded,* but beware you do not fall into the trap yourselves. Does the bird that sees the net, land in it? No! Therefore, we must see the demonic legal nets all around us, and spring these traps before the innocent get caught up in more reaping. Let those of the Spirit see in the Spirit and walk in the Spirit.

Jesus said, "Those who are not with Me are against Me." "With you? Where are You, Lord?" "I'm in the highways and the byways." "But Lord, there are thorns and thistles out there." "I know, and they are choking out the weak in heart. They hear, but don't see, because they are blinded by the ravens of life that come to steal, kill and destroy the seed along the narrow path. Help Me heal the lame and blind, raise the dead, strengthen the weak, and deliver the demoniac, so that all can go and proclaim freedom in My kingdom. *There is power in binding and loosing,* **if it were not so, I wouldn't have told you to go. Where I lead you, I will also follow. I AM with you always, I will not forsake you, be not afraid! My kingdom is taken by force. I have overcome the world, and you will also overcome it as you seek Me with all your heart, and do the will of our Father. Greater works will you do because I have gone to the Father, and the comforter has come to help you hear My voice in order to set the captives free."**

Get Violent!

Fighting is violent, and the violent take it by force. Take what? Take all that has been stolen from our Father's flock. *The sheep of His pastures are all around us.* We, like David, must violently break the jaws of these demonic lions and bears that hold their prey at bay. Prayer to our Father is as peaceful and calming as still waters are in the cool of the day, **but not warfare, it's violent.** The good thing about warfare is that the spoils are quickly received. That is why a praise report list is needed so as to record the spoils of battle and testify with evidence about the power of our God.

The Siege...talk or action?

A siege against the kingdom of hell is no threat to them if they know we are all talk. Red alert only comes on when they think we are serious about a 40-day siege. Even though each of us have our position in this siege against darkness, we are not alone. Just like Nehemiah, recruits are coming, and positions are being taken. Overcoming obstacles of threats and opposition only speed the process of time to finish the work while the day is at hand (Neh. 4). We may have started out on the defense, but the day of offensive action is here at hand. Pick up your sWORD and do the work assigned you. Plow through the rubbish of this crumbled world and build a safety zone for the innocent to find refuge. Our place on the wall is right in front of us, our lists; coupled with God's authority working through us means apocalypse for demonic powers.

The Father calls for His Adams, but Jesus calls for His Davids. Not the flute or harp player, as much as the righteous warrior that rages against the powers that enrage the Father. The battle is on. Pick up your sword and banner, and wave them high. This is the wave that everyone is looking for, because this wave of arms must come first, in order to usher in the wave of souls.

Revival is seeing, believing, and doing!

When the darkened scales fall off our eyes, we will start seeing mankind as victims. We must see how man gropes around in deep darkness, before real revival can make us truly alive again. Revival is not more flute playing, because too much music will make you sit around and cry in your, "poor me blues." Revival is getting up with a purpose in mind. His purposes with the mind of Christ! Only then will we feel useful in Christ and have a sense of worth in Him. He will show us how useful we are with Him when we mind the same desires. Our motivation to pray, worship, share, evangelize, and war, will flourish within us and radiate out because the Holy Spirit is in full reign of authority within us and through us. Joy unspeakable will bubble out of us because of His goodness in using us and making us a player on the field instead of a spectator in our seats. Players are excited and enthusiastic, dedicated and disciplined for one cause and one cause only...**WINNING!** Even though we slip and fall, getting up, overcoming, and running for the prize, will once again be our heart's desire. **Jesus only blesses what He initiates! He initiates civilians to be soldiers, and soldiers to be warriors, and warriors to be winners, not whiners. He will conquer you to bless you. Let Him!** Let Him conquer the unmerciful Saul and enthrone the sacrificing David to fight the righteous fight, and spill the blood of the demonic powers. Our treasures will be the spoils that are laid up in heaven for us. What we sow in darkness will be revealed in the light. That goes two ways. We can sow warfare against darkness and have spoils reaped in the heavenlies. Moths and rust will not harm our treasures if they are lives taken back from the jaws of darkness. There is a reward to be had, the same type of reward that Jesus had, the reward of reigning for a job well done against darkness, and the lifting of souls to the Father. Harvesting is toilsome work, picking and plucking, gathering and protecting, day in and day out, blood, sweat and tears, but it's worth it because our rest is eternal while our work is for a season.

John the Baptist was a fighter too. He waged war against the physical minds of men. He fought man's darkness in preparation for the coming Light...Christ. We too are to fight the darkness hovering over man's mind in preparation for the return of Christ. John yelled at evil and pulled no punches for fear of his own skin, and so we too must yell the battle cry and punch out the darkness that captures mankind.

There is a way that seems right unto man, but the end leads to death (Prov. 14:12). Why? Because they are blind. Upon knowing they are blind, it is our duty to help them see, with no fear for ourselves. It can be a dirty job as it was for Jesus. He even got His hands dirty as He applied mud to the blind eyes, because His motives were to help them see, so they could choose (John 9:6-39). Are we afraid of getting muddy or hurt? Jesus got both, and to the point of death and burial. Now that is both a muddy and a hurtful situation.

I wonder if grace can be grieved because of not rolling up our shirtsleeves for the job at hand. Didn't Jesus kind of roll up His sleeves and wash their feet? That's dirty too. The physical cleaning is good, but not as great as the cleansing of filth that cesspools its way into the minds of men.

Where are the John the Baptists today? Look in the mirror more closely this time and see what the Spirit sees. Have you felt lonely and been sent out to the wilderness? Does your spiritual nourishment seem to be the same old manna over and over again? **Joshua 5:11-12** says that when we invade the enemy and eat their crops, then the fruitless taste of manna will cease in our lives. New strength and deadened taste buds will come alive again as we eat and enjoy the spoils of invasions. The enemy will be paralyzed with fear if we see, taste, and possess the land. There is no turning back because the Jordan River will not dry up again. **One Way only** is the signpost for all that travel His Holy path. Distractions that hinder and smother us from self-sacrificing warfare must be circumcised and bow down to His ways. Dying to self or cutting away of self, is self-done. God does not do it for us, we must do it ourselves, as well as help others be free from the foreskins of failure. It is better to **"knife"** self now, than to put it off and later receive the sword of chastisement. There must be a cutting away from self to God. Die to self now or die later, it's solely our choice...and choose we must.

Souls watching from heaven are waiting and hoping with great expectation as they cheer on the runners of today. Greater today are the numbers of cheerleaders for us, than there were for them. We can make it too! Greater work can we do today, and greater works tomorrow. Greater the number of cheerleaders needed, so greater the battle must be, yet greater the victory! Victory, oh victory, how sweet the sound, with joy unspeakable for gathering souls all around. Oh what joys await the soul reapers when checking off the Book for lost souls that were saved. Joy awaits the church doer, not the churchgoer...as the doer is over the hearer only. Here again, the doer is not to bang his neighbor's head, but bang and bombard the **demonic heads** that hover over them. **Warfare is to war-for!** Focusing on whom to war for will motivate and empower us to war against and overcome. Too much focusing on the giants will feed fear, and cause the milk and honey in the Promised Land to spoil unused. Spoils of war are ours to be had by fighting the good fight, not for just hanging on. Crawling into heaven is not His idea of faithful soldiers, unless they are wounded doers. Being wounded is not the real casualty, it's the not going out or getting in. All fighters expect to get punched around and bruised, but our Commander will not allow us to be bruised beyond all that we can bear through Him. **He is our Red Cross** and for that Cross we must fight and protect. The lame, blind, deaf and dumb, are trying to find the Way, the Truth and the Life. How will they know how to be saved and fight, if they are not told and shown? Forty days of binding and loosing for others is far better than forty years of whining in the wilderness of self-pleasure or self-pity. These parties of pleasure and self-pity have flute songs that pacify, while warfare parties are trumpeted into battle plans. Stand up or sit down, where will we be when the music stops playing? **Sitting or standing?** Sitting is for our time of being seated with Christ, while our standing is for the day at hand, which is far spent already. Make a list! Wage a war! Fight the fight! Free the slaves! Take the spoils! Then, later on we can wine and dine with the Lamb for all eternity!

Imagine this: 1000 soldiers, each having a list of people in their world that they war over each day, with you being on each of their lists, because of being a part of their world. Wow! One thousand soldiers warring for you and I each day. Wow, again! Things would surely change in your life and in your families, without your constant focus of prayers being only for them, but for others as being more important. Our prayers will reap more power, if first sown into others. As we war to change others, we in turn will be changed. Darkness will be broken off, and the light will have freedom to shine in and save souls and restore weak lives. If every Christian soldier got into the fight by listing the people of their post, then the world would be closer to being covered over with righteous war and Holy prayer. Heavenly power could then overshadow this earth like never before possible. **If we think it probable, Jesus will make it possible.** Our list would be like the tribes in our care, tribes that represent the faithful ones.

We must bring them out of the wilderness of life, and cross them through the raging rivers that flood us. No one is exempt...**all are called**...each having a tribal position with authority and rank.

CHAPTER 6

Explanation of the Plan

The **40-day warfare plan (part 1 — list #2)** is only to be read out loud, Monday through Saturday.

The **people's names (list #1)** in your world, saved or unsaved, are to be called out only on Sunday...the day of rest and praise. In addition, on each Sunday, read out loud the pages of **the praise and proxy prayer (list #3).** This same **list #3** is used in **part 2**...40 days of praise and thanksgiving. If your people's list gets too large to read both it and the praise and proxy list, then just lay your hand on your people's list, and read the praise and proxy pages over them.

(Better understanding is coming up)

Proxy Prayers of Love

A friend of mine told me that the Jewish people do not ask anything from God on their Holy Sabbath Day. They just praise God for His goodness and for answering their six days of prayer...that sounds like a great thing that we should all be doing, hey!

I came up with this proxy prayers list after I heard about a pastor kneeling at the altar, and **saying** the sinner's prayer **in proxy** for his sister, and she got saved that next week.

We will all see the power in proxy prayer, as we enter into this dimension of caring and loving others, as more **important than ourselves.** You see...**the power**

in love is the greatest power there is. God is love, so the power itself is love. Jesus was the physical example of love, that is why He could do so many miracles. He was, and is, the Son of God, but He came as a man to show us how powerful love could be when it was rightly joined with the Father. We are to carry on the causes of love and let all see the power that follows it. Love is the power to be self-sacrificing as was Christ. He walked this walk by turning His cheek to His enemies for the sake of love, so that the power that works through love could help the needy and the hurting. To move outside of love is to move outside of the power to heal and to help. Jesus could not sacrifice or compromise the Father's love if He wanted to fulfill His Father's purpose in mankind, and be the worthy sacrifice on the cross. *Love is the beginning and the ending, and it holds everything together in-between.* Prayers birthed in love will get the quickest answers and be the greatest testimonies. Love is powerful because it turns its cheek, and absorbs hatred, bitterness, unforgiveness, rejection, accusation, and many other demonic powers that come to steal, kill, and destroy love. Love is the power that reveals God's goodness and mercy. Jesus was love, that is why He could move with such great power. The 40 days of temptations in the wilderness were for the purpose of moving Him in selfish or unselfish motives. Jesus overcame selfish temptations in order to do the Father's will and receive the power to reveal love as the very nature of the Father. Love which moves the heart of God in power, cannot be gained overnight. It is a walk of selflessness in order to manifest the power of the Word. To reveal love is to let Christ live outside of us, not just to live in us. Once He comes in us, He wants to move through us and outside of us to reveal the Father's love. **We are not the important ones. It is Jesus being let go through us that makes us fulfilled in life.**

Judge Our Motives

It is our motives behind our decisions, that judge us as being Christlike or selfish. Why do we do and say the things we do? Well, the motives behind them will reveal the truth. Jesus rebuked selfish motives from Peter, and said, "Get ye behind me Satan" (Matt. 16:23). Yes, Satan does work through believers, so stay alert to the enemy's devices, and spoil his plans over yourself as well as for others who are blind to the enemy's tricks and schemes. One simple rule of thumb for becoming more selfless is to ask yourself this question each time a decision gets in your face, **"W.W.J.D....**What would Jesus do? Or what would love do?" Your proper response to these questions will not only change you, but those who are watching you. Not everyone can stand the truth about themselves, but it will be healing and deliverance to those who can bear it. As we hold truth dearly and honestly, we can then see **selfishness** for what it really **is...sin.** The good news is that once we see it, we can renounce it, repent, and get free from it. It is not the Lord who will jump you with feelings of failure and condemnation; He only pricks your conscience in order to prompt you into repentance for your own good. He can only prick our conscience to the degree that we walk in humility and maturity, because without these we would fall prey to the accuser's guilt and condemnation. Therefore, if you cannot take correction, it is a sign of pride and immaturity. *Ouch!* The Lord's hope of changing the immature is in the process of wearing us down with more laps around the mountain. **My feet are sore...aren't yours?** We must humble ourselves or be humbled...**it is our choice,** but humbled we must become, one way or the other. This is the meaning of dying to self for Christ.

Pride vs. Humility

I have joked for years about how to be humble and proud of it, but true humility can only come as a fruit of the Spirit as we pray for it. Yes...I said, **pray for humility.** Moses was the most humble man on earth and look how God used him (Num. 12:3). If you don't pray for humility, then pride and many other spirits will slowly start building up a stronghold, which will become hard to tear down. The **real truth** is that the more pride we have, the more God resists us (James 4:6). If God is resisting us, do you think He will be using us totally or answering our prayers? *I don't think so...!* Will the Lord **anoint** a pulpit message through a person of pride, even if it is the Word? The message may be true to the Word, but it must have the anointing upon it in order to make a change in the congregation. The fruit or results will be the proof in the pudding as to whether or not it is anointed. The fruit is always the sign...just as miracle signs do follow the Gospel message. **"You younger men, follow the leadership of those who are older. And all of you serve each other with humble spirits, for God gives special blessings to those who are humble, but sets himself against those who are proud. If you will humble yourselves under the mighty hand of God, in his good time he will lift you up" (I Peter 5:5-6).**

Note: Just because I am writing this book, does not mean that I have it all together. This stuff hurts me more than it does you...*I am held accountable!* **GRACE! GRACE! O Lord!** (Luke 12:47-48).

Freedom of Choice

Freedom is His only purpose for mankind, not heaviness, and hopelessness. Knowing what the purpose is behind love will help you understand His voice more clearly over the adversary's voice of accusation. The Father's purpose is only to help and to heal, but we must wake up and see why we make the decisions that we do. We must see that our decisions are like **red lights** that we can either obey or run through. When we obey His Word, as in stopping at the red light of action, we receive His blessings by keeping the enemy at bay in our lives. However, when we are disobedient to His Word in rebellion, then we open up the doors for the demonic patrol to pull us over for a deserved ticket. We must pay for it by reaping what we sow. It is not what the Father wants for us, but **He gives us a free will to choose right from wrong.** When we call out in repentance for His mercy and His forgiveness, then He overturns the demonic judgment against us. *The MAJOR PROBLEM* against repentance is that we let the enemy accuse us as failures to the point of not going to the Father for forgiveness. Listening to guilt and condemnation, instead of grace and mercy, will open doors for shame and self-hatred to legally rule us toward destruction. **BEWARE! The adversary is searching to and fro for those to whom he can devour, and it's those who rebel against the Word of God that fall prey to the tormenter for the hope of saving their souls.** The Word is not a bunch of religious hoops that you must jump through in order to make God happy. No! It is for our benefit! It allows Him to bless us, and it allows His love to help others see and understand His love in personal ways for themselves. When we move outside of love and peace, then we move outside of His Word, and the wolves are waiting.

The Father allows the wolves to nip at our heels in order to chase us into His arms of love and forgiveness.

David Trains Against the Lions and the Bears

The stray sheep in David's pasture were his biggest problem. That is how he became proficient in using his sling. *His sling, like the Word of God,* was used to hurl a stone of bruising size at its designated target, in order to scare the rebellious stray back into the flock for submission and protection. It was **his persistence** in swirling the sling that strengthened his arms to swing the sword against his enemies, as well as to club the lions and bears (1 Sam. 17:34-37). Being faithful in the small exercises of faith and endurance that seem so mundane and monotonous, will some-day become useful in **slaying the giants that hinder God's purposes and plans.**

Could doing this list be a GIANT in your life?

It was David's love for the sheep that made him put his life on the line to save the rebellious as well as the innocent. The bears and the lions were just doing what came natural to them, and they probably did it very well many times before David took over his father's flock from his brothers. I'm sure David rose up with righteous anger and said, **"Enough is enough"**...and *this **must** be our attitude as well.*

We are to be Davids today that will stand in the gap between good and evil with love, and say, **"No more, no more, N.O....M.O.R.E.!"** Our Lord will let us see the enemy, just like David saw, and then ask us these words, **"What are you going to do about it?"** It's up to us, like it was David. Sure God could have smote the bear, the lion, and even Goliath, but He didn't. We must stand up in the righteous anger of love, and fight against injustice no matter what the cost. That is why warfare intercession is not just about prayer, it's standing in the gap between right and wrong, and saying **"No more...enough is enough, I command you in Jesus' name to get away and never return again."** Our natural wars were to help those who could not help themselves. *It is still the same today in the Spirit, as it was with David in the natural.*

Warfare is to war...for. We must war for the innocent and against the demonic bullies in the airways. We have more with us than there are with them, if we just see with the eyes of Elijah (II Kings 6:16-17). Besides, only **one-third** of the angels fell with Satan, that leaves **two-thirds** with us. The deck is stacked against them, and we are the **Key Holders** that were given dominion here on earth to bind and to loose. Way too much has been stolen already. Now is the time to make up for lost ground, and to take back all that has been lost and stolen by our ignorance and unbelief. **We are perishing for lack of knowledge and so are those in our care.** Our focus must change, and turn back from self-fulfillment in order to help, to heal, to protect, and to give rest to the weak and weary. We must build a perimeter around the innocent and hold back the enemy's attacks, so that they can get free from deception and receive with understanding and clarity of mind, the whole truth about God's love for themselves. The battle is in our faces and the victory is in our hands, if we will just be willing to pick up our cross and wheel our sword in defiance to demonic tyranny, cutting and severing the ropes of bondage that hold the innocent in captivity.

The Father says...   **"I desire to set My people free.
Who will wheel My power for their
Victory?"**

This high calling has always been there for those who will incline their ears to His plea for helpers. Me? Help God? Of course! Why do you think He saved you, just for your soul? No! He needs our help to rule out His will here on earth as we will rule with Him in heaven (Matt. 25:21).

Revelation 2:26-27: "To every one who overcomes — who to the very end keeps on doing things that please me — I will give power over the nations. You will rule them with a rod of iron just as my Father gave me the authority to rule them...."

It is His power and His strength, but it is our **willingness to *yield*** to His Spirit and do the greater works than Jesus did. Greater works by means of there being more of us doing the Father's bidding, and holding our positions on the wall. The little foxes spoil the vines, and it is time for us to stop up the cracks in the walls on our post and rebuke the spoiler.

We have to get mad!

I'm getting mad just typing this, and you should too.

> **M...ad**
> **A...t**
> **D...emons**

Here Is More Understanding About the Plan

I am using Round 2 as an example, so that this plan can be easily understood. (A detailed page of dates is coming up.)

> **Round 1 is...January 1-May 1, skip May 2**
> **Round 2 is...May 3-August 31**
> **Round 3 is...September 1-December 31**

Today is **May 1,** the last day of hands off!
Praise God.

Tomorrow is **May 2,** the day that we skip over since it is a break day that fits in-between the first 120-day siege.

May 3 will be the first day of warfare again.

(Round 2), identical to **January 1-May 1 = (Round 1).**

However, if you need a break from all this stuff, then do so, **it is not a law!** If you feel good about another round, then go for it, because there will be people starting this at different times. **The main thing is...are you seeing VICTORIES in people's lives?** You should be seeing changes to the point of new excitement for more warfare. I know that this is meant for some to do continually, by caring for others all the time. Some will reap a **hundredfold,** some **sixtyfold,** some **thirtyfold,** and some only **twofold,** *but there definitely will be an increase for those who toil* (Matt. 13:23, 25:15).

Positive action of sowing in faith with the Lord will reap a harvest of plenty. No matter how small or how great the harvest may become, the good news will be that of going forward. The **"Well done, thy good and faithful servants,"** will be said to those who try, not those who don't.

Round 2 of 120 days of warfare, praise, and hands off, will be done in the same way as Round 1. This 120 days will end on August 30. Then there is one break day on August 31. Then, Round 3 will begin on September 1.

December 31 will complete one full year of warring for the people in our world. The results should be many. Your spoils list should be full of testimonies of how God has moved in lives all around you, not to mention the changes that you don't hear about. The many you hear about are just a small number in comparison to the big picture. We will not see the whole picture which warfare affects until we get to heaven. Our rewards will be totaled then, and **it will be surprising.**

It's never too late to jump into this plan!

The rewards will be the same, just like the story in...**Matthew 20:10,** where the farmer hired workers at different times of the day and they all got the same pay. Even-though this story is really about salvation, **a workman is worthy of his hire,** and each will be greatly rewarded (Matt. 10:10).

It's never too late!
Start today!

Becoming a Brave Heart

One thing is for sure, those of you who engage in this warfare plan will become stronger in faith, and more bullheaded about the things of God. Your prayers will have more authority and **you will see them answered more readily.** Deliverance will become a reality in your walk with the Lord as you see more demonic walls fall down in people's lives through your diligence. Your diligent march around Jericho's walls will cause them to tumble down (Josh. 6:2).

You will not give into negative feelings so quickly, because the eyes of your understanding will be open and clear. Sickness and disease will be enemies with less hold on those you love. Your prayers of intercession will be more intense. You will walk with more freedom from guilt and condemnation because of new insight about how the spirits work. You will feel the joy of working with the Lord in one accord, instead of feeling like you are in the way. Boldness will rise up in your soul, and determination will strengthen your countenance.

The bottom line is, that you will become more fulfilled through the realization of doing something positive for the causes of Christ.

The BIGGEST LIE that you will hear is...
"Wait until tomorrow."
"It's not important enough to do it today, tomorrow will be okay, you will be better devoted to it then."
B.u.l.l....lony!

This lie causes me pain because I have a list of unattended things that are left undone as most of us have. ***The pathway to hell is paved with excuses, and wallpapered with tomorrow's good intentions.*** Today is the day of salvation, not just salvation of our souls, but salvation for lost and undone things that need salvaging into new life. The bird in the hand of today is better than two birds in the bushes of un-promised tomorrows. **Children of the Light...work while it's light (that's today),** not in the dimly lit tomorrows that we can only see through a glass darkly. **Work in the day, which is already far spent. Today is the Day of Salvation and...**

FREEDOM FROM COMPLACENCY AND FAILURE.

Stand up and stomp your foot on the head of those snakes that bite at your Achilles' heel. Your walk has been crippled long enough; limp no more....

Run...Run...and Run some more!
Run Forrest...R.U.N.!

CHAPTER *7*

Dates and Plans

*T*hese are the dates and procedures for each part and their lists.

There are 3 Parts, 4 Lists, and 3 Rounds.

Dates...are the times when we agree together in one accord.
Parts... (part 1) 40 days of Warfare
(part 2) 40 days of Praise
(part 3) 40 days of Hands Off
which equals one, 120-day Round

Rounds...120 days equal one Round. There are three Rounds per year,
plus five skip days.

Lists...are the 4 LISTS used in each part...
list #1, your list of people
list #2, warfare, demons and commands (Part 1)
list #3, praise and proxy prayers (Part 2)
list #4, your spoils list
No list...Hands off (Part 3)

Please photocopy DATE PAGE
and mark on calendar

Warfare dates...Part 1
Jan. 1-Feb. 9, May 3-June 11, Sept. 1-Oct. 10

Praise dates...Part 2
Feb. 10-Mar. 2, June 12-July 21, Oct. 11-Nov. 19

Hands off dates...Part 3
Mar. 22-May 1, July 22-Aug. 30, Nov. 20-Dec. 30

5 skip dates
Easter Sunday, May 2, Aug. 31, Dec. 25 & 31

Round 1 120 days....beginning of year

40 days of warfare...Jan. 1-Feb. 9
40 days of praise...Feb. 10-March 21
40 days of hands off...March 22-May 1
Skip dates...Easter Sunday & May 2

Round 2 120 days...mid-year
40 days of warfare...May 3-June 11
40 days of praise...June 12-July 21
40 days of hands off...July 22-Aug. 30
Skip date...Aug. 31

Round 3 120 days...end of year
40 days of warfare...Sept. 1-Oct. 10
40 days of praise...Oct. 11-Nov. 19
40 days of hands off...Nov. 20-Dec. 30
Skip dates...Dec. 25 & Dec. 31

That is 3 Rounds of 120 days, and
5 skip days, which = 365 days

In Jesus' name.
I bless the works of your hands, and the
words of your mouth, and I *bind* and
rebuke any and all assignments sent out
against you. *No weapon* formed against
you shall prosper. Be strong! Be brave!
Fear not!

NOTE: There is *GREAT POWER* in speakig out loud this plan with others in the same room. When my wife and I do it together, we both yawn out stuff. But GREATER PERSONAL DELIVERANCE happens when we read it together with more people in the room. Try to do it with others, if possible. I cannot imagine what would happen if a whole church did it together. I would love to see it happen!

NOTE: Even though Matthew 18:18-19 does talk about binding a brother in error, Jesus also says that ANYTHING we agree on, as well as BIND, will be done! I think He is willing to apply this to demonic powers...don't you? Matthew 12:29-30...bind Satan first.

PART 1

40 Days of Warfare
Binding and Loosing List #2

Remember to make two lists: *your people's list (#1) and your spoil's list (#4).*

Photocopy these pages for yourself and for your partners as well, so that continual use of this book will not ruin it from future reading.

Once again...
read these pages (LIST #2) out loud Monday-Saturday over your #1 people's list.

On Sunday just read the praise and proxy list #3 over your people. On your spoils list #4, record all things happening, good or bad, to your people. Add more names as you SEE more problems in people.

The Scriptures are to better your understanding as to how I came up with some of my beliefs. You do not have to quote them unless it strengthens your faith.

It will always help you to pray in the Spirit before starting.

Mornings seem best, but I've had to *start* it as late as 11:59 p.m.

If you should miss a day, just say, *"Grace, Grace, in Jesus' name,"* and continue on with it.

Your hope will rise to new levels each day you try.

PART 1 LIST #2 START HERE

JAN. 1-FEB. 9, MAY 3-JUNE 11, & SEPT. 1-OCT. 10

40 DAYS OF WARFARE
BINDING AND LOOSING

Commission Scripture: Isaiah 49:9, TLB: "Through you I am saying to the prisoners of darkness...come out! I am giving you your freedom!"

I am a child of God, because I am born again through the blood of Jesus Christ...saved by His grace alone, and not by my works of righteousness. I am seated in the third Heaven with my Lord Jesus Christ, raised up into new life by His resurrecting power.

Heb. 12:22-24, Eph. 2:8

I repent of all sins and unforgiveness, which would hinder my prayers and authority. *Repent and forgive here!*

Matt. 18:34-35, Mark 11:25-26

I am crucified with Christ...it is no longer I that lives, but Christ lives in me to fulfill the Father's will in my life, as well as in the lives of those around me. Rev. 12:11, Gal. 2:20, Matt. 5:44

Greater is He that is in me, than he that is in the world. No weapon formed against me will prosper, because my Father has placed His Angels in charge over me and has sealed me unto the day of redemption. He has adopted me into His family by the blood of Jesus. Luke 10:19, 1 John 3:8, 4:4 & 5:4, Eph. 1:5, Psalm 91:11

I am filled with His Holy Spirit and with His anointing power to do good works, to preach His salvation, to speak with new tongues, to cast out demons, to lay hands on the sick, and *they will be healed in Jesus' name.* Mark 16:15-18

This authority is not by my might nor by my power, but by the Holy Spirit, the Blood of Jesus and by the Word of God...in Jesus' name. Zech. 4:6, Rev. 12:11

Jesus said I could receive anything I ask for in His name; and even greater works would I do because He returned to the Father. The Holy Spirit makes daily intercession for me. Signs and wonders do follow me as I boldly proclaim the day of salvation to the lost.   John 14:12-14, Romans 8:26

I bind all demonic forces here on earth as they are bound in heaven, and I loose the Holy Spirit upon these people with wisdom and understanding, so that they can make a clear, free will choice...for righteous judgment.
                              Rev. 16:7, Psalm 48:10 & 119:34-37, Prov. 2:6-7, Matt. 18:18

I will fear no evil or any deadly poisons that try to attack me, because I put on the full armor of my God, who supplies all my needs according to His riches in Christ Jesus.
                                    Romans 13:12, Eph. 6:11, Phil. 4:19, Luke 10:19

I am a joint-heir with the Father and the Son...we are one in the Spirit. A threefold cord is not easily broken. I have been made to be more than a conqueror. My cup overflows with every spiritual blessing that my Father is able to give me through Christ Jesus; not a drop...not a trickle...not even a river, but a f-l-o-o-d! Pressed down, shaken together and running over!
                    Luke 6:38, 1 Cor. 2:9, Gal. 4:7, Psalm 23:5, Romans 8:17, John 14:20, Ecc. 4:12

And I will give unto you the keys to the kingdom of heaven, and whatsoever you shall bind on earth shall be bound in heaven, and whatsoever you shall loose on earth shall be loosed in heaven.   Matt. 18:18-20

And that if any two or three shall agree as touching anything here on earth, our Father shall give to those who ask, and Jesus will be in our midst to perform His will.   Matt. 16:19-20

By the authority of the Word of God, the principles of binding and loosing, and of agreement in prayer, I hereby command all you demon spirits to be bound, rebuked, and cast out of all the people on my lists, and on my prayer partner's lists, which cover

70

every person listed and their bloodlines (descendents), their spouses and their bloodlines back to ten generations on both sides of their families...*in Jesus' name!*

Deut. 23:2-3, 1 Peter 2:9, Isa. 55:4-5, Matt. 10:1 & 22:39,
Acts 2:39, 11:14 & 16:31, Mark 3:15, Luke 10:17, Romans 13:9

All you demons have been placed under the feet of our Lord Jesus Christ, who rules in your midst and to whom all knees must bow.

Psalm 110, Eph. 1:22, Gen. 3:15

We ask our Father to send out warring angels to cast you demons out with the name of Jesus and to apply His blood upon your victims...to pierce you with the same blood-covered spear that you used to pierce Jesus...your swords shall now enter your own hearts, because Jesus has taught our fingers to make war. In Jesus' name, we now strip you of all your weapons and we break your bows into pieces.

Heb. 1:14, Psalm 37:14-1, Matt. 13:41, Luke 10:18-19

We call upon the stone that the builders rejected, which is Christ the Rock to fall upon you foul spirits, crushing you to pieces, scattering your dust to the wind. Lord, continue flashing your fearful arrows of lightning, routing out the enemy, while raining down fire and brimstone on these wicked spirits, scorching them with burning wind.

Psalm 11:6 & 18:14, Matt. 21:42-44, 1 Cor. 10:4

We loose the fire of Elijah to burn up all demonic chaff in these people's lives; and we send the blood of Jesus in like a flood tide to push back all demonic forces separating darkness from the light, *setting their victims free indeed.*

1 Kings 18:38, Psalm 21:9, Psalm 104:4, Isa. 59:19, 2 Sam. 5:20, Matt. 13:41-43

Let all demons reap torture just as they tortured the martyrs and be cast into the pit of Tartarus, the deepest part of hell. You will not manifest in these people again, except to come out and go where Jesus sends you, or to the abyss, and never return again.

Luke 8:31, Matt. 13:41-42, Gal. 6:7

We take our place as the sons and daughters of God, to claim our inheritance of executing the vengeance of God upon all the wicked spiritual rulers of this present age.

We first bind you Satan (the strong man) and all your power off these people with the authority vested in us through Jesus Himself, and no other! Psalm 149:7, Eph. 6:12, John 10:10

Since the violent do take the kingdom by force, we ask You, Holy Spirit, to manifest righteous anger through us against spiritual wickedness. Matt. 11:12

We war not against flesh and blood, but against principalities, against powers, against the rulers of the darkness of this world, and against spiritual wickedness in high places. Eph. 6:12

We bind all evil spirits sent out on assignments to steal, kill, and destroy these people's lives. With the Word of God as the two-edged sword in our mouths and tongues, we bind your kings, Satan, with chains, and your nobles and demons with fetters of iron. Psalm 149:6-9 & 107:14,16

You demons have *no legal right* or ground to reside in these bodies, because Jesus Christ obtained your order of eviction 2,000 years ago at Calvary. This power of authority stands continually around the clock, because it is W-R-I-T-T-E-N and S-I-G-N-E-D by Jesus Himself in His own Blood. Gal. 3:17

We ask You, heavenly Father, by Your Son, Jesus Christ, to send forth angelic sheriffs to execute this order of eviction! You demonic spirits *must vacate* God's property now, or be forcibly removed. This is the last warning today that you will receive. Psalm 103:20-21, John 16:23-24, Matt. 13:41-43

We demand you to loose your victims n-o-w, in Jesus' name!

In Jesus' name, we break all generational curses on both sides of our families, back to Adam and Eve that would interfere with our future happy marriages, families, descendants and ministries. We specifically break curses of illegitimacy, which may be upon anyone that we stand in proxy for on our lists.   Zech. 3:2

Our Lord Jesus Christ rebukes you, Satan.

We renounce and rebuke every legal hold, doorkeeper, ground and right, that any demons claim they have in our lives. We bind and command all connected, related, familiar or associated, and resulting demons to leave *n-o-w*...in Jesus' name.

Again, we *bind* you first, Satan. We *bind* and *rebuke* you as the Lord of flies. We *bind* and expose you as the father of lies. We *bind* the prince of darkness. We *bind* the prince of death. We *bind* the prince of destruction. We *bind* all princes and principalities. We *bind* all spirits of pride and bondage, and *command them to leave now...in Jesus' name!*

Heb. 2:14-15, Matt. 12:29-30, 10:25, 12:24, John 8:44, Rev. 9:11

Fear: We command fear and all these spirits associated with fear to leave *now,* in Jesus' name!

Fear of: Animals, snakes, insects, mice, storms, thunder, lightning, fire, floods, earthquakes, tornadoes, hurricanes, the sun, darkness, phobias, claustrophobia, agoraphobia, necrophobia, suspicion, paranoia, distrust, fear of man, rejection, confrontations, loneliness, disappointments, poverty, success or failure, fear of making wrong decisions, fear of missing God's will, cowardice, intimidation, shyness, speech impediments, stuttering, stammering, fear of public speaking, competition, words spoken by us or by others, worry, stress, anxiety attacks, nervousness, flinching, panic, terror, trauma, horror, shock, tormenting spirits, fear of dying, driving, accidents, being a victim of a crime, falling, pain, drowning, fear of mental illness, sickness, diseases, aging, fear of Holy Spirit manifestations, fear of Satan and his demons, fear of curses and deliverance.

Lying, Criticism: We command all spirits of lying to leave now, in Jesus' name!

Lying spirits, white lies, forked-tongue, promise breaking, false accusation, accusing of the brethren, faultfinding, falsehood, blaming, criticism, judgmental, slander, scoffing, mockery, back-biting, comparison, gossip, telephone busybodies, talebearer, tattletale, idle chatter, unbridled tongue, bickering, division, false responsibility, false burden, unsanctified mercy, spirit of condemnation, false guilt, false logic, misconception, negative thinking-speaking, pessimism, presumption, pretense, pretentious acts, hypocrisy, two-faced, unholy acting-playing-joking, foolishness, cursing, foul language, coarse jesting, deceiver, manipulator, deception, self-seduction, self-deception, manipulation, brown nose, suck-up, political, cheating, kickbacks, bribery, blackmail, sting, swindle, sham, betrayal, unfairness, unreliable, usurper, trespasser, thief, stealing, lawlessness, double-mindedness, compromise, indifference, confusion, indecision, doubt, dubious, unbelief, denial, lack of faith, vacillation, irresolute, procrastination, putting it off, I'll get around to it someday, hesitate, in just a minute.

We command all spirits of physical and spiritual deafness, blindness, and darkness to be broken off our minds, bodies, spirits, and souls right now, in Jesus' name.   Isaiah 35:3-6

Pride: We command all these spirits of pride to leave *now,* in Jesus' name!

Rebellion, defiance, insubordination, stubbornness, tenacious, undermining, rebel, outlaw, seared conscience, hard-hearted, stiff-necked pride, the seven heads of leviathan, arrogance, haughtiness, blame-shifting, obnoxious, indignant, lofty thoughts, mockery, noble, pious, pomp, smug, self-righteousness, false compassion, false pride, false humility, lack of humility, conceit, know it all, vanity, macho man, egomania, favoritism, cliques, exclusivity, respectability, man-pleasing, prejudice, racism, redneck-Yankee mentality, importance, high-mindedness, opinionated, performance drive, over competitiveness, perfectionism, religious traditions, Pharisee, Sadducee, religious formality and prayers, denominational pride, Jezebel-

Ahab spirit, humanism, mind science, human reasoning, soulish prayers, self-will, spoiled, my way, my, I, me, Legion, unholy independence, self-centeredness, self-justification, narcissism, self-exaltation, self-awareness, selfish ambition.

All Addictions: We bind and rebuke all addictions in Jesus' name.

Addictive behavior, bad habits, dependency on prescription medicine, drug addiction, nicotine addiction, tobacco, caffeine, sugar, sweets, soft drinks, food, alcohol, TV, books, music, buying or shopping, work or sports, pornography, sex, internet.

Enslaving Habits and Excesses: We command these and all other spirits of excess to leave *now*, in Jesus' name!

Drunkenness, smoking, tobacco-chewing, nail-biting, gluttony, overeating, slow metabolism, eating disorders, purging, bulimia, binging, anorexia nervosa, water retention, excessive calories, excessive fats, excessive sleeping, excessive talking, chatter box, head running, gambling, greed, excessive spending-buying, covetousness, possessiveness, materialism, excessive sports-playing-entertainment, over-competition, perfectionist, hyperactivity, drug abuse—legal or illegal, lust, nymphomania.

Temptation: We break the powers of temptation, and command them all to leave *now*, in Jesus' name!

Ungodly music-books-movies-games-toys-newspapers-TV shows and ungodly money making, gambling, materialism, lust of the eyes, unholy relationships, pornography, lust, pride of life, covetousness, fame and fortune, recognition, urgent and compulsive drives, gluttony, worldly dancing, rhythmic spirits, alcohol, drugs.

By the authority in Jesus' name we bind all demonic activity off...our families-godly relationships-friends-enemies-marriages and future spouses, our property-possessions-vehicles-finances-jobs-time-business-work and play, gardens and crops, animals-pets, our churches-ministry callings, schools, bodies-minds-spirits and souls.

We bind all evil spirits that cause struggle for power and position, ambition, self-exaltation, Babylon, and unholy competition, and all spirits that prompt people to answer "yes" or "no" too quickly or thoughtlessly. We bind presumption, compulsion, loose tongue, unbridled emotions, ungodly spontaneity, blasphemy, name calling, unclean speech, coarse jesting, and impulsive behavior.

Hindering Spirits: We bind all hindering spirits and command them to leave *now,* in Jesus' name!

All spirits that hinder...fasting, dieting, energy, strength in body, thyroid function, proper metabolism, appestate, appropriate use of time, orderliness, decision-making, memory, concentration, spelling, reading, learning, communication, speech, travel, forgiveness, joy, peace, humility, wisdom, submission, truth, justice, holiness and purity, financial provision, buying-selling, liquidation, godly friendships, receiving love, expressing affection, prayers-repentance-conviction and salvation, deliverance, Bible reading, praise-worship, effectual ministry.

Evil Assignments, Missions: We command all spirits sent out on missions as assignments to be canceled, and we sever all transmissions and command them to be of *no effect,* in Jesus' name.

Spirits causing blindness-darkness and cloudiness to the Gospel, no fear of God, all perceived strengths, self-wisdom, lack of wisdom and understanding, ignorance, stupidity, deception, defrauding, the devourer, Legion, corrupt communications, financial lack, theft, indebtedness, welfare dependency, job restrictions, poverty, accident proneness, bodily attack, vehicle problems, laziness, tiredness-fatigue, oversleeping, slumbering, complacency, lack of energy-initiative and willpower, lack of devotion, backsliding, lack of commitment-submission, carelessness, neglect, irresponsibility, trash, filth, rust, decay, pack rat syndrome, hermit syndrome, escapism, separation, divorce, Asmodeus, unholy relationships-soul ties and marriages, unlovable, hiding, running away, introvert, vagabond, bad morals, poor ethics.

We rebuke any and all other demonic assignments
and transmissions in Jesus' name!

Emotional: We command all spirits attacking the emotions to leave *now,* in Jesus' name!

Shame, embarrassment, self-hatred, lack of self-worth, nobody, inferiority complex, no one likes me, no one loves me, self-rejection, depression, oppression, manic-depressive disorder, heaviness, sadness, despair, hopelessness, aimless wondering, broken heart, misery, sorrow, unnatural grief over the loss of loved ones, despondency, shyness, fear of rejection, intimidation, rejection, not wanted, insecurity, abandonment-discard, withdrawal, victim mentality, desolation, slavery, wounded spirit, loss of true self, fifth wheel, outsider, don't fit in, unstable, disunity, uncertainty, floundering, left-field, loneliness, emptiness, failure, self-pity, impatience, edginess, intolerance, restlessness, irritability, frustration, selfishness, self-centeredness.

Mental Attacks: We command all spirits striking these people mentally to leave *now,* in Jesus' name!

Insanity, schizophrenia, split or multiple personalities, craziness, madness, deranged, nervous breakdown, psychosis, neurosis, tormenting memories, senility, mind-binding spirits, mind control, loss of mind, dumb, hysteria, hallucinations, confusion, duh, dullness of comprehension, unteachableness, deception, dyslexia, forgetfulness, mental retardation, isolation, displacement, mental bondage, intellectual pride, doubt and unbelief, evil thoughts, evil plotting, treachery, intimidation, gates of hell in the mind, bands of iron.

Emotional-Mental Attacks Combined: We command all spirits that attack the emotions and the mind simultaneously, to leave *now,* in Jesus' name!

Unforgiveness, holding grudges, resentment, bitterness, hardened heart, hatred, strife, anger, rage, overaggressive, lashing out, contention, argument, turbulence, short temper, fighting, quarreling, feuding, violence, cruelty, threatening, physical abuse, verbal abuse, child abuse, yelling, screaming, roaring, tumultuous, overreactive, carousing, ridicule, sarcasm, contempt, spitefulness, oppressiveness, belittling, jealousy, complaining, whining, murmuring, defensiveness, irrationality, criticism, judgmentalism, anxiety, vengeance, retaliation, hostility, malice, frustration, ugliness, offensiveness, disturbance, distortion-disintegration of personality, hypochondria, inner agony, anguish, sleep loss, insomnia, nightmares, haunting memories and dreams, snoring, bruxism-grinding teeth, tormenting spirits, effects of anesthesia, starvation for love, touch-me-not, heaviness, gloom, passivity, false burdens, false responsibilities, unrighteous judgment, over-compulsion to confess, self-martyrdom, confrontation with honesty at all cost, hatred of men or women.

Sexual Oppression: We bind and rebuke all demonic spirits that attack people sexually and we demand them to leave *now,* in Jesus' name!

All forms of sexual sin, all unholy sexual activity, adultery, fornication, premarital sex, masturbation, sexual lust, uncontrolled passions, wanton-roving eyes, flirtation, seduction, debauchery, depravity, dissipation, demon sex (incubus-succubus), sexual perversions, lesbianism, homosexuality, sodomy, Queen Bee, Butch, bisexual, transsexual, transvestite, effeminacy, mannishness, impotence, frigidity, suppression of normal desire, fantasy lust, sensual love, prostitution, harlotry, nymphomania, whoremonger, pimp, striptease, go-go dancer, exotic dancer, voyeurism, exposure, streaker, flasher, sadomasochism, erotic sexual behavior, bestiality, orgies, promiscuity, child molestation, pedophile, incest, rape, porno houses and stores, porno books-videos-films-pictures and literature, sexually transmitted diseases.

All Genetic Defects: We bind and rebuke all defects in Jesus' name.

Dwarfism, Down's syndrome, spina bifida, birth defects, cleft palate, club foot, hemophilia, deviated septum, in utero effects of radiation-drug addiction and smoking.

All Reproductive Afflictions: We command all these spirits of afflictions to leave *now,* in Jesus' name.

Hormonal disorders, chemical imbalance, female problems, pre-menstrual syndrome (PMS), irregularity, issue of blood, meno-pause problems, toxemia, infertility, sterile, miscarriages, barren womb, breast cancer, uterine cancer, fibroid tumors, cervical cancer, enlarged prostate and cancer.

All Bone and Joint Ailments: We command all spirits causing these ailments to leave *now,* in Jesus' name.

All types of arthritis, fibromyalgia, hip problems, back pain, osteoporosis, spinal problems, scoliosis, bone disease, bone cancer, leukemia, broken bones, slipped-ruptured or herniated discs, knee problems, foot pain, bone spurs, bunions, tooth decay-cavities-gingivitis-pyorrhea-periodontal disease, bone loss, dry sockets, all teeth and gum problems, abscesses, plaque and mercury.

All Nerve and Muscle Disorders: We bind and rebuke all these spirits, and command them to leave *now,* in Jesus' name.

Polio, palsy, neurological dysfunction, Parkinson's disease, prolonged pain, pinched nerves, twitch, tic, pulled or torn muscles and tendons, hernias, plantaris, muscular dystrophy, multiple sclerosis, paraplegia, numbness, lameness, maimed, halt, quadriplegia, all crippling diseases, Lou Gehrigs-A.L.S., epilepsy, spasm, cerebral palsy, Bell's palsy, sciatic nerve blockage.

All Respiratory Afflictions: We command all these spirits to leave *now,* in Jesus' name.

Asthma, hay fever, hypersensitivity, allergies, colds, sinus congestion, sinus infection, emphysema, bronchitis, lung cancer, lung disorders, shortness of breath, whooping cough.

All Digestive Disorders: We command all these spirits to leave *now,* in Jesus' name.

Excessive gas, acid stomach, ulcers, nausea, motion sickness, esophageal reflux, heartburn, fire, liver ailments, cirrhosis of the liver, gallbladder disorders, gallstones, kidney stones, colon-rectal cancer, colonic polyps, impacted colon, Crohn's disease, diverticulosis, colitis, constipation, diarrhea, hemorrhoids, spleen-kidney-bladder-infections-poisons and malfunctions, bladder reflux, all poisons and toxins.

All Brain-Sensory Ailments: We rebuke and command all these ailments to leave *now,* in Jesus' name.

Migraines, headaches, dizziness, fainting spells, blackouts, all brain diseases, amnesia, autism, A.D.D. syndrome, learning disabilities, Alzheimer's, brain damage from drugs and overdose.

All Diseases and Afflictions: We bind, rebuke, and command all these spirits to leave *now,* in Jesus' name.

Spirit of infirmity, Apollyon the destroyer, autoimmune disease, immune deficiency, acquired immune deficiency syndrome (AIDS), human immunodeficiency virus (HIV), all infections, all viruses, measles, chicken pox, mumps, tonsillitis, strep, mononucleosis, all forms of hepatitis, malaria, fevers, chills, flu, pneumonia, rheumatic fever, tumors, all types of cancer, cysts, metabolic disorders, fibrocystic disease, Hodgkin's disease, cellulite, dropsy, unnatural perspiration, phlebitis, all circulatory and blood afflictions, Raynaud, varicose veins, heart attacks, strokes, aneurysm, mitral valve prolapse, angina, abnormal heart conditions, arterial blockage-plaque, arteriosclerosis, high or low blood pressure, hypertension, diabetes, hypoglycemia, high cholesterol, psoriasis, dandruff, skin fungi and cancer, leprosy-Hansen's disease, shingles, lupus, athlete's foot, Candida albicans, diphtheria, A.L.D., acne pimples, dry skin, rashes, itching, scratching, hives, scars, untimely wrinkles-disfigurement-tattoos and body piercing, warts, insect bites, bee stings, snake bites, poison plants, deafness, hearing loss, tinnitus, ringing in ears, inner ear infection, mute spirit, all eye problems, blindness, cataracts, glaucoma, impaired and blurred vision, pink eye, eye-ear-nose and throat problems-infections and irritations.

Death: We command all spirits associated with death and destruction to leave *now,* in Jesus' name!

Suicide, murder, abortion, barren womb, killing, assassination, hit man, civil war, anarchy, revolt, mutiny, terrorism, arson, accidents-injury-maiming-torturing and afflictions, destruction, apocalypse, chaos, small death, stalking, rape, kidnapping, sinister, martial arts, karate, obsession with darkness and black, necrophilia, all tormenting spirits.

Curses and Occult: We bind and command all curses and occultic activity to be severed by the name of Jesus and by the power of His blood. Curses and every related oppressing spirit must leave *now,* in Jesus' name.

Curses from the womb, all generational-ancestral and environmental curses, reactionary sins of fathers, familiar spirits, controlling spirits, antichrist, soul power of man, counterfeit spirits, false anointings-prophecy-tongues and false gifts, unholy use of anointings and gifts, selling and abusing spiritual gifts, divination, mysticism, sorcery, Gypsy, fortune-tellers, mediums, necromancy, poltergeist, seances, curses, hexes, vexes, wizardry, horoscopes, conjurations, ritualism, palm reading, incantations, spells, charms, potions, jinxes, crystal balls, Ouija boards, tarot cards, tea leaves, dungeon and dragons, Pokémon, trances, hypnosis, snake charming, water witching, mesmerize, levitation, astral projection, extrasensory perception, clairvoyance, graphology-automatic handwriting and analysis, all psychic powers-readings and healings, therapeutic touch, fire-walking, transcendental meditation, mental telepathy, chanting, yoga, mantras, unholy sacrifices and vows, reincarnation, superstition, walking under ladders, Friday the 13th, luck, coincidence, amulets, rabbits foot-medals-articles and actions used for luck (luck is short for Lucifer), Ying and Yang, unholy holidays, Halloween, bewitchments, black magic, white magic, pentagrams, voodoo, occultism, legerdemain, witch doctors, root doctors, dispatching demons, PWCCA, spiritism, ruling spirits, Mague IV, spirit-guide, masters, channelers, strongman, witchcraft, witches, warlocks, wizards, Lucifer worship, satanism, demon worship, human sacrifice, occult-satanic-psychic-books-music and artifacts, other gods, idolatry, graven images, secret societies and vows, Masonic Lodge type groups, Freemasonry, Shriners, Socialism, Communism, Marxism, Fascism, Legalism, Klu Klux Klan (KKK), white supremacist groups, anti-Semitism, pantheism, atheism, new age doctrine, human philosophies, Church of Wicca, Dark World, extraterrestrial deceptions, Buddhism, Islam, Hinduism, Shintoism, Jehovah's Witness, Mormonism, Moonies, Hari Khrisna, Christian Science, Bahai, all Babylonian spirits from the Roman Catholic system, religious spirits, saint and priest idolatry, worship and veneration of Mary, genuflecting, Holy Water, religious sacraments.

We catch the thieves and demand them to return *sevenfold* of all things they have stolen from us in Jesus' name!   Prov. 6:31

We also strip you of all your spoils.   Ex. 12:36

We use God's mighty weapons to knock down the devil's stronghold, and these falling walls will loose the people from darkness into finding Christ with obedience.   2 Cor. 10:3-6

We plead the blood of Jesus over every person on our lists and ask You, Father, to loose the hounds of heaven in Jesus' name, to go and round up all these lost souls, and lead them into Your kingdom, and place their names into the Lamb's Book of Life.

Please, Lord...post warring angels as a hedge of protection with the blood of Jesus around every person in order to hold back all demonic attacks and influences, and restore the fragments of their souls that were stolen through unholy soul-ties.

No *weapon* formed against us will prosper, and our God will burn every weapon, because our Commander of the Heavenly Armies is here among us to rescue us in Jesus' name.

Isaiah 54:17, Psalm 46:9,11

Our strength to conquer with mighty power is only because You smile on us with favor, O Lord. We trust in Your weapons alone.

Psalm 44:3-7

Jesus, please loose us from all shame, and allow us to eat from Your tree of life through faith, hope and love...in order to set the captives free for Your Holy pleasures.

Holy Spirit, please baptize us in Holy fire with radical Christianity as it was in the first days of Pentecost.

For this purpose, the Son of God was manifested that He would destroy the works of the devil. He did then, and He is still destroying the devil's works today.   1 John 3:8, 1 Thes. 5:18

All power is given to execute these orders of binding and loosing through united praying and steadfastness...because of the name of Jesus and His precious blood!

So Let Us Praise the Lord in All Things!

For it is written...it is finished...the battle is over...in Jesus' name. Amen...Amen...and A.M.E.N.!

These are just extra Scriptures.
You can add more of your own.
Acts 10:3, Col. 2:15, Luke 11:20, Mark 16:17-18,
Isaiah 14:12-17, Ezek. 28:17-19, Rev. 12:11, 20:11,
2 Cor. 10:4-6, James 4:7

Add any demonic spirits' names that I have missed.
You are free to add or take away, it's not a law!

NOTES

NOTES

PART 2 LIST #3

40 Days of Praise and Proxy Prayers
FEB. 10-MARCH 21, JUNE 12-JULY 21, & OCT. 11-NOV. 19

I praise You, Lord Jesus, for loosing these people on our prayer lists from all demonic spirits that Satan has sent out against them. I thank You for the power in Your Blood that sets man free in his emotions, his physical body, his attitudes, his mental state, family, friends, and possessions. Warfare prayers have opened doors for warring angels to go in and deliver people from a host of evil powers that reign in the airways all around us.

You are awesome, O Lord Jesus, Your goodness never ceases. Your loving eyes and hands are always there for us with tender mercies and grace. Your forgiveness and patience is continually poured out over us because of who You are in us, and because of the love You have for the Father. Thank You, Father, for sending Jesus to die on the cross and pay the price for our eternal salvation. Because of His Blood sacrifice we can face all our tomorrows with joy unspeakable and full of glory.

Your glory is our joy, O Lord, and setting us free from demonic powers breaks the yokes of bondage that have held us, our friends, relatives, and our enemies. Your light has broken the powers of darkness off the minds of man, so that they can clearly see Your love, and are then able to make a clear decision to follow You or not. Your judgment is always just, so I praise You for Your fair dealings with mankind.

I thank You with a grateful heart for trusting me with this list of people that You have placed into my world for safekeeping. There is no power in myself, no might in my strength, and nothing good will ever come forth as being Holy, unless You, Holy Spirit, continue to move and create in man the Father's will. I have warred for these people in faith that Holy angels have been casting out demons from people's lives with the power of Jesus. Souls have been saved and more are in the process.

86

Christians are waking up from their slumber and putting on their armor to fight the good fight of faith. My trust is totally in You, Lord Jesus, because You are the only power that can help and save mankind. Evil is raging all around us, but Your Power and Your Blood has put up a siege wall against all darkness of the airways. All princes and principalities have been bound by Your authority that You have vested into Your servants.

I will praise You Father, for a Holy 40 days of devotion, for what Your Spirit has done for these people in our world. The time of binding and loosing is over for now, just like six days of working. This is the time to rest, rejoice, praise, give glory, and be thankful for all that You have done, and are continuing to do. You are on the throne, having everything under control. I am so glad to know You, and for having been chosen by You to be Your child that once was lost, but now am found.

I am grateful beyond what mere words can express for what You are doing in these people's lives, their bloodline, their spouses, and their bloodline back to ten generations on both sides of their families, as well as my prayer partners and their lists, all because of the name of Jesus. I thank You, Jesus! I thank You, Holy Spirit, but most of all, I thank You, Father, for being the Great I AM, and for grafting us onto the tree of life. There is no way to repay You, except for being obedient to Your call, to its highest point.

Please anoint us for greater obedience!

The Baptism of Your Holy Spirit is the only answer for these people. Please, Lord, fill them fully so they can taste and see how wonderful You really are. Help them to open the door of their hearts to let You in. Move on them, Lord, in ways that are miraculous, so they can realize the depths of Your love. Call them by name, steady their hands and feet, and fill their hearts with Your presence, while protecting them from the accuser and his demon powers. Help these victims to be victorious for Jesus. Let the doorways and windows of revival open wide, and spill out upon these innocent sheep. Forgive all their sins, and bless them with Your Spirit of Grace, Mercy, and Power. They have no help outside of You, O Lord. I am asking You and thanking You for setting them free indeed. Nothing is impossible for You, Lord Jesus, that's why I am praising You for the power and might of Your Blood as it comes in like a flood tide to flush out all demonic trash and float it away into the bottomless pit. Thank You for sending the fire of Elijah that burns up all idols and demonic chaff in people's lives. I'm glad to know by faith that all these powers that have been trespassing in the Temple of the Holy Spirit are being tormented by the Word of God, and pierced with the torturous swords that are dipped in Your Blood and used by warring angels.

Thank You, Jesus, that Your anointing on prayer, praise, warfare and deliverance, all have their place in Your kingdom. I am believing that this 40-day program of binding and loosing, and then 40 days of praising You for deliverance and healing, is and was designed by You for all of us to do. The fruit grown upon this tree is evident to all that this is of God and not of man.

Thank You, Holy Spirit! Praise You, Jesus, and Glory to You, our Father!

It is finished! The battle is over!
In Jesus' name! Amen and AMEN.

Proxy Salvation

Jesus, I stand in proxy for all of the people on these lists. I will repent for them, and ask You to come into their lives as Savior and Lord. This salvation plea is for them, and I ask You, Lord, to call them into the reality of this prayer, and forgive all their sins. I ask You to come in with the Holy Spirit's Baptism, while releasing Your Spirit of repentance upon them.

O Lord, *please hear* these people and their bloodline, their spouses, and their bloodline on both sides of their families...say this prayer....

"Lord Jesus, I am a sinner. I repent of all my sins and I ask You to forgive me for every one through the blood sacrifice that You paid on the cross. I ask You, Jesus, to come into my heart and never leave me. Please baptize me in Your Holy Spirit with fire, so that I will preach your Gospel with Holy Boldness. I dedicate the rest of my life to serving and following You and Your Word, and every DESIRE of the Holy Spirit.

"Use me, my Lord Jesus, Your will be done, but not mine. Fill this body, Your temple, with Your resurrection power, so that Your presence can be seen in me, and draw all men unto Yourself for salvation. Save me...use me...and I will thank You, Jesus, as my Lord and my Savior. Amen and Amen!"

Lukewarm Christian - Proxy Prayer

My Lord Jesus, please forgive me as I repent of all my sins and for being lukewarm to You. Hear me along with all the people on these lists. Refill us with Your Holy Spirit, with fire and boldness, so that we can do the works that have been assigned us by the Father. Help us, Father, to lift up Your Son, so that all of mankind can see His love and salvation power.

I have been neglectful of Your high calling and gave way for compromise and complacency to take root in place of my heart's first love. I became cool to Your will and voice. Reestablish my heart and feet on the road that leads toward Your perfect will. Reveal Your Word to me in new revelational depths. Fill me with Your love and compassion for others.

Help me to put on the Holy armor daily and fight the good fight of faith, setting the captives free. Let prayer to You and warfare against the enemy be what pulsates through my bloodstream and bloodline. I sacrifice myself on the altar of self-death, so that my praise and thanksgiving will be an offering pleasing to You, my Lord and Savior, Jesus.

Jesus, You are the Christ, the Son of God, and the Holy Lamb. Thank You for dying, so that I can live. Holy Spirit, help me empty myself of me, so that I can be filled with You. Fill me with Your presence that I might know Your power, that I might know Your glory, and that I might know the precious anointing of Your Spirit. Fill me with Your fire for radical boldness, so that I can be used to preach Your Gospel message and demonstrate Your healing and deliverance power, in order to set the captives free.

I plead the Blood of Jesus over all these people on my list and their bloodlines on both sides of their families. I ask that we all be washed and cleansed anew while being anointed with Your fresh oil...in Jesus' name!

Amen...Amen...and A.M.E.N.!

PART 3

<u>NO LIST, HANDS OFF</u>
MARCH 22-MAY 1, JULY 22-AUG. 30, & NOV. 20-DEC. 30

The Word does not return void.
Rest in the faithfulness of the Lord.
He will keep that which is entrusted to Him.
He cares for the sparrows...how much more, the lost.
We will Praise You, O Lord,
In All Things.

"Thank You!"
"Thank You!"
"Thank You!"

This is not the end...but the beginning!

Much more needs to be said, but let it be said in my next book. This is the time to be doing, not just talking about it.

My **next book** will have more teaching, as well as being comprised of testimonies of victories won and ground taken, so send me your testimonies as well as your names for my prayer list.

> **God Bless you all! You are important and needed far more than you know or understand!**

See you soon, or see you up there!

P.S....
    Always remember...
                  LIFE is just a TEST...
                                Pass It!

Videotapes are available on deliverance for self, as well as for others.

Please notify us if we can help you in anyway. You can come to us, or we can come to you. Lord willing!

Ask, seek, and knock!

P.S. The Squeaky Hinge Gets the Oil!

> *MAY JESUS BLESS YOUR PRAYERS, AND GIVE YOU THE DESIRES OF YOUR HEART...Psalm 37:4*

Daniel and Sheila Brothers
180 Ball Park Rd.
Lexington, S.C. 29072

803-359-6468
Fax 803-359-1258
Email...the 40daybook@hotmail.com

Glossary of Terms

Abscess - accumulation of pus in body tissue.
A.D.D. syndrome - attention deficit disorder.
Agoraphobia - fear of crowds or open places.
Ahab - weak, compromise, double-minded, puppet.
A.L.D. - Adrenoleukodystrophy, hereditary disease of children. Research Hospital-800-352-9424
A.L.S. - muscle weakness involving spinal cord.
Amnesia - loss of memory.
Amulet - charm to ward off evil or bring fortune.
Aneurysm - abnormal dilatation of blood vessels.
Angina - attack of painful spasms.
Anorexia nervosa - eating disorder, becoming fat.
Anti-Semitism - Jew haters and discrimination.
Apocalyse - universal destruction or disaster.
Apollyon - Rev. 9:11, Greek word for Satan; destroyer.
Appestat - area of brain that controls appetite.
Arteriosclerosis - abnormal arterial walls.
Asmodeus - prevents marriage; Jewish demonology.
Astral Projection - project body to another location.
Autism - pervasive developmental disorder.
Autoimmune disease - body stops producing antibodies.
Babylon - spirits of excessive wickedness.

Backbiting - to attack character or reputation.
Bands of iron - mental confinement or prison.
Bell's palsy - paralysis of the face.
Bestiality - human sex with animals.
Binging - excessive eating or drinking.
Bladder reflux - flowing back in the bladder.
Bronchitis - inflammation of bronchial tubes.
Brown nose - to seek favors by flattery.
Bruxing - to grind teeth.
Bulimia - overeat disorder, then vomit.
Butch - woman having male traits.
Candida albicans - yeast-fungus infecting the skin.
Carousing - to engage in drunken revel.
Cerebral palsy - brain condition effecting muscles.
Channelers - a person spirits converse through.
Civil War - internal strife and division.
Clairvoyance - seeing beyond the natural vision.
Claustrophobia - fear of closed-in places.
Cleft palate - deformity in roof of mouth.
Club foot - foot deformity.
Colitis - inflammation of the colon.
Communism - government rules society by force.
Contention - strife, conflict, or dispute.
Coarse jesting - vulgar joking.
Confrontation with honesty at all cost - driven to confess without regard
     of who or what it hurts.
Conjurations - calling on demons to cause action.
Crohn's disease - irritable bowel syndrome.
Debauchery - indulge in sensual pleasures; orgies.
Defrauding - to deprive.
Depravity - state of being evil and corrupt; wicked.
Deranged - to make insane.
Desolation - devastation, ruin.
Deviate septum - pulling away of cavity walls.
Devourer - totally consume.
Diabetes - high levels of glucose in blood.
Diphtheria - mucous membrane disease.
Displacement - being driven away.

Dissipation - given to immoral conduct; intemperance.

Diverticulosis - saclike herniations in the colon.

Divination - practice of fortune-telling.

Dropsy - body tissue contains too much fluid.

Duh - dull, blank, lack of comprehension.

Effeminacy - feminine traits in males.

Egomania - excessive to one's self.

Emphysema - disease of the lungs.

Epilepsy - disorder of the nervous system.

Esophageal reflux - stomach gases resurface.

Familiar - similar spirits in people or places.

Extrasensory perception - supernatural communication.

Extraterrestrial - life on other planets; UFO.

Fascism - prejudice dictator Hitler mentality.

Fibrocystic - fibrous tumor.

Fibromyalgia - chronic pain in muscle around joints.

Fifth wheel - unnecessary or unwanted person.

Fire - name of spirit that causes burning sensations.

Floundering - to struggle helplessly, to falter.

Forked tongue - to tell lies.

Frigidity - orgasm failure in women; cold to sex.

Gates of hell in the mind - demonic doorways in mind.

Genuflecting - bending of knee to worship. Used in idolatry of wrong worship.

Graphology - study of handwriting and analysis.

Halt - to be lame or limp.

Hemophilia - blood fails to clot.

Hepatitis - inflammation of the liver.

Hernias - protrusion of organ in abdominal wall.

Hexes - practice of witchcraft, casting spells.

Humanism - human affairs more important than God.

Hypersensitivity - excessively sensitive.

Hypertension - extreme nervous tension.

Hypochondria - excessive attention to one's health.

Hypocrisy - falsehood between beliefs and actions.

Hypoglycemia - low glucose in the blood.

Idolatry - worship of anything other than "The God."

Impotence - penis erection failure for intercourse.

Indifference - without interest or concern.
Incantation - chanting of words to invoke magic.
Incest - sex within blood relatives.
Incubus - sex with male spirits.
Introvert - shy and self-focus.
In utero - within the uterus.
Irresolute - doubtful; unsure of opinion.
Jezebel - domineering, controlling, manipulative.
Jinxes - a spell to bring bad luck.
Kickback - refund portion of illegal profit.
Left field - position out of the ordinary.
Legalism - salvation through works, rules, and laws.
Legerdemain - sleight of hand-trickery-deception.
Legion - title given to, "We are many."
Leprosy-Hansen's - destruction of skin tissue.
Leukemia - cancer of bone marrow.
Leviathan - sea serpent of pride, rebellion.
Lou Gehrig's - A.L.S.; muscular spinal cord weakness.
Lupus - ulcerating skin disease.
Mague IV - honorable priesthood in third legion.
Malaria - diseases caused by parasites.
Malice - desire to inflict harm.
Manic depressive - causing alteration in moods.
Mantras - Hindu chanting of words.
Marxism - theory of a classless society.
Metabolism - where body energy is produced.
Mononucleosis - lymphoid tissue disease.
Multiple sclerosis - crippling of nerve and muscle.
Muscular dystrophy - gradual wasting away of muscle.
Mitral valve prolapse - heart valve contractions.
Mysticism - spiritual thought of unknown mysteries.
Narcissism - excessive self-love, vanity.
Necromancy - communicating with the dead.
Necrophilia - erotic attraction to corpses.
Necrophobia - abnormal fear of dead bodies.
Neurological dysfunction - malfunction of nerves.
Neurosis - personality disorder causing anxiety.
Nymphomania - abnormal sexual desire in female.

Oppression - to weigh down, suppress, burdensome.

Orgies - unbridled sexual group parties.

Osteoporosis - brittle bones due to loss of calcium.

Ouija board - game board used in séance.

Overcompulsion to confess - being driven to confess without regard of who it hurts.

Palsy - condition of paralysis.

Pantheism - belief that God is the universe.

Parkinson's disease - chronic nervous disease.

Paraplegia - paralysis of lower limbs.

Pedophile - adult's sexual desire for children.

Periodontal - tooth bone loss disease.

Pessimism - negative attitude.

Phlebitis - blood circulation restriction.

Pimp - sells prostitutes.

Pious - self-righteous and critical.

Plantaris - a muscle in the calf.

Pokémon - toy game that opens doors for demons.

Poltergeist - manifestation of spirits by noises.

Pomp - vain display of dignity or importance.

Promiscuity - having numerous sexual partners.

Pretentious acts - outward show of pretending.

Pride of life - self-worth of worldly gain.

Psoriasis - scaly inflammation of skin.

Psychosis - hallucinations; delusions.

Purging - forcing self to vomit meals.

Pwcca - messenger demon for Satan.

Pyorrhea - tooth gum disease.

Quadriplegia - paralysis below the neck.

Queen Bee - woman of perverted sexual rank.

Raynaud - blood circulation restriction.

Reactionary sins of father - bloodline curses.

Redneck-Yankee mentality - prejudice pride.

Rheumatic fever - inflammatory fever.

Rhythmic spirits - erotic rhythm.

Roaring - loud deep sound.

Sadomasochism - sexual gratification through pain.

Sciatic nerve blockage - largest nerve in the body, blockage causes paralysis.

Scientific remote viewing - seeing into the past, present, and future. Actually feel as if you are there.

Scoliosis - curvature of the spine.

Séance - a meeting to communicate with the dead.

Senility - mental infirmity of old age.

Sensual - lacking sexual moral restraints.

Shingles - painful skin eruption.

Sinister - threatening or planning evil.

Slander - false statement of others.

Slow metabolism - slow production of energy.

Small death - dying inside, but not life itself.

Smug - superiority, over-confidence.

Socialism - similar to Communism, but without force.

Sodomy - anal and oral sex.

Soul power of man - controlling and manipulation.

Soul-tie - joining oneself with person or things.

Spina bifida - defects in spinal canal.

Spiritualism - converse with spirits through mediums.

Sterile - unable to have children.

Sting - illegal operation.

Strongman - ruler of authority; prison guard; Satan.

Succubus - sex with female spirits.

Talebearer - one who spreads gossip.

Tenacious - persistent, stubborn and obstinate.

Thyroid function - gland regulating growth.

Tinnitus - ringing in ears.

Toxemia - blood poison from toxins.

Toxins - bacterial poisons attacking blood cells.

Transcendental Meditation - Hindu meditation.

Transsexual - having a sex change by surgery.

Transvestite - to dress as the opposite sex.

Tumultuous - disorderly, highly agitated, distraught.

Turbulence - violent, disorder or commotion.

Ugliness - threatening trouble or danger.

Unsanctified mercy - give mercy when you shouldn't.

Usurper - illegal seizure; take by force.

Vacillation - indecisive; waver in mind; unsteady.

Vagabond - wanderer, nomad, tramp, vagrant, unsettled.

Vexes - curse assignment to torment, provoke trouble.
Voyeurism - sexual gratification by visual actions.
Wanton eyes - lustful, desirable glare.
Water witching - it opens door to spiritualism.
Whoremonger - a dealing or trade of whoring.
Wicca - witchcraft from pre-Christian religion.
Yin Yang - Chinese symbol that influences destiny.

p. 11 - Quite an assumption

p. 12 - another unusual interpretation

p. 19 - .1st binding Satan - p. 19
(also see Mt. scripture - p. 15

p. 23 - sweeping idea about
use of Psalms today

p. 37 - Good questions

p. 42 - innocent victims (?)